GOSPEL AND KINGDOM

A Christian Interpretation of the Old Testament

Also by Graeme Goldsworthy

THE GOSPEL IN REVELATION:
Gospel and Apocalypse

GOSPEL AND WISDOM:
Israel's Wisdom Literature in the Christian Life

GOSPEL
AND
KINGDOM

*A Christian Interpretation
of the Old Testament*

GRAEME GOLDSWORTHY MA, ThD

paternoster press

British Library Cataloguing in Publication Data

Goldsworthy, Graeme
Gospel and kingdom.
1. Bible. Old Testament – Criticism,
interpretation, etc.
I. Title
221   BS1171.2

ISBN 0–85364–608–2

Typeset by Photoprint, Torquay, Devon
and Printed in the U.K. for
THE PATERNOSTER PRESS
P.O. Box 300, Carlisle, Cumbria, CA3 0QS
by Cox & Wyman Ltd, Reading, Berkshire

Contents

Preface   7
Introduction   9

1. Why read the Old Testament?   13
2. Bridging the gap   22
3. What is the Old Testament?   30
4. Biblical theology and the history of redemption   39
5. The covenant and the kingdom of God   44
6. The kingdom revealed in Eden   49
7. The kingdom revealed in Israel's history   56
8. The kingdom revealed in prophecy   74
9. The kingdom revealed in Jesus Christ   84
10. Principles of interpretation   99
11. It's that giant again!   103
    Conclusion   109

Appendix A: Suggested readings   111
Appendix B: Questions for group or private study   113
Appendix C: Passages for interpretation   116

Index   120

Preface

THIS BOOK HAS GROWN OUT OF A DEEP CONCERN FOR THE RECOVERY of the Old Testament as part of the Christian Bible. It is indisputable that even evangelical Christians demonstrate a neglect of and an ignorance towards the first three-quarters of the Bible. We need not reflect here on the cause of this problem, but that it is a problem hardly needs to be stated. One could almost suggest that 'Bible-believing' Christians suffer a bad conscience over this serious lack of understanding of the Bible as a whole – and with good reason.

I have often been asked to give a series of studies on the Old Testament by various groups. 'We haven't done anything on the Old Testament for a long time. What about a series on the minor prophets?' (The minor prophets seem to have a peculiar fascination for study groups which are ignorant of the Old Testament!) I have usually responded with a counter-proposal that we hold a series of studies on the structure of the Old Testament theology and the unity of the Bible. Not surprisingly, the outcome has usually been an enthusiastic response to anything which helps to show how the various parts of the Bible hang together.

While teaching a course of biblical theology over a number of years at Moore Theological College I found it almost impossible to recommend a single book (of an introductory kind) on the subject. Obviously what was needed was something for the pastor and teacher, as well as for the ordinary Christian, which would give basic principles of Christian interpretation of the Old Testament. The frequent requests by students for recommended books was from time to time replaced by a pointed challenge to undertake my own work for publication based upon the course of lectures given at Moore College.

This little book is the outcome. In writing it I have tried to keep in mind the needs of all those who, with little or no formal training, undertake the task of reading the Bible for their own edification or in order to teach others also. Experience would suggest that pastors and preachers are also in need of help of a fairly uncomplicated and non-technical kind. The risks of over-simplification are very great, but the pressing nature of the task makes such risks worth taking.

I owe a debt of gratitude to my many teachers who have instructed me in biblical and theological studies. I am particularly beholden to Archbishop Donald Robinson for imparting to me some of his enthusiasm for and insights into the study of biblical theology. I am also grateful to those who willingly helped with the typing of the manuscript.

Graeme Goldsworthy
Brisbane

INTRODUCTION

Killed Any Good Giants Lately?

THE SUNDAY SCHOOL ANNIVERSARY SERVICE HAS JUST BEGUN AND THE hall is packed with children under the watchful eyes of teachers and parents. They all sing lustily with the help of an accordion and a couple of guitars, while the song-leader conducts energetically from the platform. The children's eagerness for the Bible story soon to be presented is not shared by the young man sitting on the platform and nervously thumbing through his assorted illustrations and flash-cards. Perhaps more thoughtful than most, he is seized by a sudden doubt about the application he intends to make from the Old Testament story he is about to tell. There is nothing wrong with his visual aids, and his story-telling technique is recognized to be of a high standard. There is something which bothers him. How is he to take those far-off events of a thousand years or more before Christ and make them say something to his youthful hearers of the twentieth century?

This uncertainty is not a sudden thing. Let us suppose our friend (call him Ken) is someone who has been brought up in a Christian home and a live, Bible-based church. Over the years he has been well taught the contents of the Bible and has learned a way of applying these to his own Christian existence, assumed to be the only 'proper' way. As a Sunday School teacher he gradually acquired a skill in this kind of application, but was never quite sure of the principles behind the method. But through an interest in biblical studies he began to be aware of the variety in the literature of the Bible as well as of the historical context of its events. Not that he shared the doubts of some of the books he read as to the inspiration of the Bible, but he did become aware of the rather haphazard approach to both the original meaning of the text and to its application to the 'here-and-now' which he previously accepted.

The invitation to speak at the anniversary service has faced Ken with a new problem. He cannot simply rehash the story in accordance with the lesson material of their Sunday School curriculum (not that he was very happy with it anyway!). His uneasiness about the method of telling a Bible story was intensified a couple of weeks previously when he listened to another speaker at a children's rally present the story of David and Goliath. It had been well done and the children loved it. There had been lots of excitement in the play-acting of that great victory by God's chosen leader, and the use of visual aids had been carried out with care and precision. But Ken was most troubled by the way the speaker had applied the story. The fellow dressed up as Goliath had progressively revealed a list of childhood sins by peeling cardboard strips off his breastplate one by one, as the speaker explained the kind of 'Goliaths' we all have to meet. Then a strapping young David had appeared on cue, and produced his arsenal – a sling labelled 'faith' and five stones listed as 'obedience', 'service', 'Bible reading', 'prayer' and 'fellowship'. The speaker had omitted to say which stone actually killed Goliath, a matter which caused a little mirth when Ken discussed the talk with some friends. But underneath the mirth was a real sense of uneasiness and confusion over the matter of how such an Old Testament story should be applied.

Ken was troubled by all this because, six months ago, he would have done exactly the same thing. But now as he prepares to take the platform he is very unsure about it all. He has come to appreciate more of the historical unity and progression of the biblical events. Somehow the ingenious jumps from Goliath to our sins, from David's weapons to our faith and Christian virtues and, more significantly, from David to ourselves seems at the one time both logical yet arbitrary. Any wonder Ken is still troubled. He is about to give a talk which leans heavily on the same kind of approach and which seems to say something valid without clear reasons for its validity.

*   *   *   *   *

This story could be written a thousand ways to fit your situation and mine. If you are not a Sunday School teacher, you are a camp counsellor, a holiday Bible club helper, or maybe just an ordinary Christian struggling with the question of the relevance of the Old Testament to your Christian life. Or you are a Christian parent who wants to lead your children towards a sense of the meaningfulness of the Bible, and towards a maturity in the handling of the text of Scripture. Every time we read the Bible we meet this problem of the *right* application of the text to us, the meaning of the ancient text to today's world.

This book has been written to help bridge this gap. In order to build a bridge that will link this ancient world to modern man, we must know what manner of gap separates us. This is not an easy task, but we must make a start. If we believe that even children can learn to understand something of God's way of speaking to them through the Bible, then we must accept a life-long calling to increase our understanding of God's word so as to build surer bridges.

This book aims to provide a basic structure upon which to build a more confident use of the Old Testament, and thus of the Bible as a whole. It is intended to help Christians cross the deep ravine that separates them from the original meaning of the biblical text. It does not tell the whole story of biblical theology, but offers an invitation to begin the exciting task of reading the Bible as a living whole.

CHAPTER ONE

Why Read the Old Testament?

BEFORE COMMENCING TO BUILD OUR BRIDGE, WE MUST ASK A MORE BASIC question: why bother bridging the gap in the first place? For many Christians, the problem is not how to read the Old Testament but *why* it should be read at all.

WHY SOME PEOPLE DON'T READ THE OLD TESTAMENT

Some people still are influenced by the intellectual climate of the nineteenth century, which did much to undermine a positive appreciation of the Old Testament. The philosophical stand-point of the time led people to conclude that the Christian religion, as found in the New Testament, was nothing more than the natural evolution of man's ideas about God. Consequently the Old Testament was regarded as a primitive, and therefore outdated, expression of religion. It was seen not only as being *pre-Christian* because it failed by several centuries to be concerned with the events of the gospel, but also as being *sub-Christian* because it failed to reach the ethical and theological heights of the New Testament. Yet many people who are quite unaffected by such ideas about the Old Testament may in practice adopt a similar attitude. For they see it as no more than a background to the teaching of the New. Perhaps they would refuse to downgrade the theological import-ance of the Old Testament because of their convictions about the inspiration and authority of the whole Bible. But in practice such people can be even more neglectful of the Old Testament than other Christians are, who do not hold such a high view of inspiration.

Ironically, the evangelical view of scripture itself can make the problem worse. For the 'evolutionist' is happy to dismiss as crude and primitive those parts of the Old Testament which he finds morally offensive. The 'conservative', on the other hand, has to find some way of reconciling his view of the Old Testament as the word of God with such things as . . . Israel's slaughter of the Canaanites, the cursing of enemies in some psalms, or the wide prescription of capital punishment in the law of Moses. Even if parts of the Old Testament do not appear morally reprehensible to the 'conservative' Christian, other parts appear to be completely irrelevant.

For a third group of people, the problem with the Old Testament is simply that on the whole they find it dry and uninteresting; it is wordy, cumbersome and confusing. Whatever their view of scripture, the sheer weight and complexity of this collection of ancient books (more than three times the bulk of the New Testament) leads to boredom, apathy and neglect rather than deliberately thought-out rejection.

There is a simple way to avoid these difficulties. Our consciences are less likely to prick us for the neglect of the Old Testament if we are giving ourselves to the study of the New! After a while the Old Testament drops right out of sight and that does not cause us any pain at all.

WHY OTHER PEOPLE *DO* READ THE OLD TESTAMENT

Happily there are people who still read the Old Testament. Their conviction that the Old Testament is part of God's written revelation is no doubt partly responsible for this. Also, if it is interpreted correctly, the Old Testament yields much to interest both young and old. Children's speakers and designers of Sunday School curricula are amongst the most consistent users of the narratives of ancient Israel for they contain a wealth of excitement and human interest to capture the imagination of children of all ages. Tell a good story about one of Israel's battles and you can have the kids on the edge of their seats! Yet pit-falls abound for the teacher who wants to draw out a Christian message from the Old Testament, though they may not be apparent until the unity of the Bible is understood.

FALSE TRAILS

Failure to recognise the unity of Scripture led some of the early expositors to follow false trails. The emergence of the allegorical method of interpretation in the early church provides a good example. Because much of the Old Testament was seen as unhelpful or sub-Christian, the only way to save it for Christian use was to distinguish a hidden 'spiritual' sense, concealed behind the natural meaning.

Allegory seemed to be a legitimate method of interpretation because it was controlled by the content of the New Testament or, later on, by Church dogma. What was lacking, however, was the kind of control the New Testament itself applied when it used the Old Testament. Instead the relationship between the natural meaning of the Old Testament and the teachings of the New was left to the ingenuity of the expositor. One serious effect of the allegorical method was that it tended to hinder people from taking the historical or natural sense of the Old Testament seriously.[1] Nor did this problem exist only for the Old Testament. In the Middle Ages the logic was taken a step further. Not only was the 'unhelpful' natural sense of the Old Testament given its spiritual sense from the natural sense of the New Testament; even the natural sense of the New Testament was seen to require its own spiritual interpretation, which was found in the tradition of the church.[2] Thus authority now lay, not in the natural meaning of the canon of Scripture, but in the teachings of the church as it interpreted the spiritual meaning according to its own dogma.

[1] See Beryl Smalley, *The Study of the Bible in the Middle Ages* (University of Notre Dame Press, 1964), Chapter 5. Stephen Langton (died 1228) applied the allegorical and spiritual interpretation with vigour. For example II Kings 1: 2 – Ahaziah fell through the lattice in his upper chamber in Samaria and lay sick – signifies a church prelate who enters hastily into the perplexities of his pastoral charge and falls into sin. Boaz in the Book of Ruth is made to represent God. When he enquires of the reapers 'Whose maid is this?' (Ruth 2: 5) he is enquiring of the doctors of theology concerning the status of the preacher who gathers sentences of Scripture for his preaching. A modern example of allegorical exposition with very great similarities to the mediaeval method of interpretation is to be found in W. Ian Thomas, *If I Perish I Perish* (Grand Rapids: Zondervan, 1967). The author deals with the Book of Esther and makes Ahasuerus represent the soul of man, Haman the sinful flesh, Mordecai the Holy Spirit, and Esther the human spirit.

[2] See J.S. Preus, *From Shadow to Promise* (Cambridge, Mass.: Harvard University Press, 1969).

FIG. 1 THE PROCESS OF SPIRITUALIZING

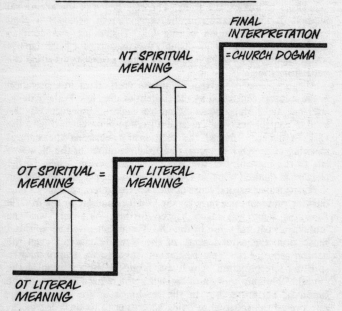

The Middle Ages saw the development of interpretation according to the four meanings of Scripture:

(a) the literal or natural meaning
(b) the moral reference to the human soul
(c) the allegorical reference to the church, and
(d) the eschatological reference to heavenly realities.

Not all texts were read with four meanings, and there was considerable activity in the field of biblical studies (especially from the 12th to the 15th centuries) as scholars sought to give proper place to the literal meaning.[3]

[3] A useful introduction to the subject of interpretation is found in R.M. Grant, *A Short History of the Interpretation of the Bible* (New York: Macmillan, 1948).

FIG. 2 THE MEDIEVAL FOUR-FOLD METHOD OF INTERPRETATION

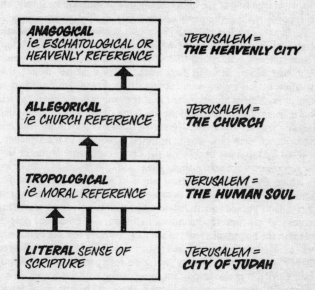

ANAGOGICAL *ie* ESCHATOLOGICAL OR HEAVENLY REFERENCE — *JERUSALEM =* **THE HEAVENLY CITY**

ALLEGORICAL *ie* CHURCH REFERENCE — *JERUSALEM =* **THE CHURCH**

TROPOLOGICAL *ie* MORAL REFERENCE — *JERUSALEM =* **THE HUMAN SOUL**

LITERAL SENSE OF SCRIPTURE — *JERUSALEM =* **CITY OF JUDAH**

THE REFORMATION PATH

It was the Protestant reformers who helped the Christian church see again the importance of the historical and natural meaning of Scripture, so that the Old Testament could be regarded as having value in itself. When the reformers recovered the authority of the Bible they not only reaffirmed a biblical doctrine of the church and salvation, but also a biblical doctrine of Scripture. Protestant interpretation was based upon the concept of the *perspicuous* (clear and self-interpreting) nature of the Bible. By removing an authority for interpretation from outside of the Bible – the infallible Church – the reformers were free to accept and see the principles of interpretation that are contained within the Bible itself.

So the self-interpreting scriptures became the sole rule of faith – *Sola Scriptura* (Scripture alone) was a rallying-cry of the Reformation. The right of interpretation was restored to every believer, but this did not mean that the principles of interpretation found within the Bible could be overlooked and every Christian follow his own whim. The allegorical method became far less popular, because the historical meaning of the Old Testament was found to be significant on its own, within the unity of the Bible.

Perhaps we understand the Protestant position better in the light of the other great principles which emerged at the Reformation. The reformers maintained that salvation is a matter of *grace alone*, by *Christ alone*, through *faith alone*. 'Grace alone' meant that salvation is God's work alone unconditioned by anything that man is or does. 'Christ alone' meant that the sinner is accepted by God on the basis of what Christ alone has done. 'Faith alone' meant that the only way for the sinner to receive salvation is by faith whereby the righteousness of Christ is imputed (credited) to the believer.

What had this got to do with the Old Testament? It meant that the reformers were establishing a method of biblical interpretation in which the natural historical sense of the Old Testament has significance for Christians because of its organic relationship to Christ. God's grace seen in his dealings with Israel is part of a living process which comes to its climax in his work of grace, the gospel, that is in the historical events of the Christ who is Jesus of Nazareth. Just as it is important to assert that this Old Testament 'sacred history' or 'salvation history' must be interpreted by the Word, Jesus Christ, it is also important to recognise that the gospel is God acting in history – more specifically, through the history of Jesus.

Mediaeval theology had internalized and subjectivized the gospel to such an extent that the basis of acceptance with God, of justification, was no longer what God did once for all in Christ, but what God was continuing to do in the life of the Christian. This *de-historicizing* of what God had done once and for all in the gospel went hand-in-hand with the *allegorizing* of the history of the Old Testament. The Reformation recovered the historical Christ-event (the gospel) as the basis of our salvation and, in turn, the objective importance of Old Testament history. This is, of course, a very different thing from the modern approach of seeing the Old Testament as part of the historical development of man's religious ideas, or as merely a background history to the New Testament age. Basically, the Old Testament is not the history of *man's* developing thoughts about *God*, but the whole Bible presents itself as the unfolding process of God's dealings with man and of his own self-disclosure to man.

IS THE OLD TESTAMENT FOR ALL CHRISTIANS?

The most compelling reason for Christians to read and study the Old Testament lies in the New Testament. The New Testament witnesses to the fact that Jesus of Nazareth is the One in whom and through whom all the promises of God find their fulfilment. These promises are only to be understood from the Old Testament; the fulfilment of the promises can be understood only in the context of the promises themselves. The New Testament presupposes a knowledge of the Old Testament. Everything that is a concern to the New Testament writers is part of the one redemptive history to which the Old Testament witnesses. The New Testament writers cannot separate the person and work of Christ, nor the life of the Christian community, from this sacred history which has its beginnings in the Old Testament.

It is, of course, of great significance that the New Testament writers constantly quote or allude to the Old Testament. One estimate is that there are at least 1600 direct quotations of the Old Testament in the New, to which may be added several thousand more New Testament passages that clearly allude to or reflect Old Testament verses.[4] Of course not all these citations show direct continuity of thought with the Old Testament, and some even show a contrast between Old and New Testaments. But the over-all effect is inescapable – the message of the New Testament has its foundations in the Old Testament.

Contrary to what is sometimes suggested, the New Testament writers were not in the habit of quoting texts without reference to their context. In fact a quotation is sometimes intended to prompt the recall of an entire passage of Old Testament scripture. For example, Paul's quotation in I Corinthians 10: 7 of part of Exodus 32: 6 refers to the festivities of the Israelites. The intention is to bring to mind the whole narrative of Israel's idolatry and the golden calf.

A person may become a Christian without much knowledge of the Old Testament. Conversion does, however, require a basic understanding of Jesus Christ as Saviour and Lord. The Christian cannot be committed to Christ without being committed to his teaching. It follows that Christ's attitude to the Old Testament will begin to convey itself to the Christian who is carefully studying the

---

[4] Henry M. Shires, *Finding the Old Testament in the New* (Philadelphia: Westminster Press, 1974), p. 15.

New Testament. The more we study the New Testament the more apparent becomes the conviction shared by Jesus, the apostles and the New Testament writers in general: namely the Old Testament is Scripture and Scripture points to Christ. The manner in which the Old Testament testifies to Christ is a question that has to be resolved on the basis of the New Testament, since it is the New Testament which provides the Christian with an authoritative interpretation of the Old.

The effect of this is twofold. As Christians we will always be looking at the Old Testament from the standpoint of the New Testament – from the framework of the gospel which is the goal of the Old Testament. But since the New Testament continually presupposes the Old Testament as a unity we, who are not acquainted with the Old Testament in the way the first Christians were, will be driven back to study the Old Testament on its own terms. To understand the whole living process of redemptive history in the Old Testament we must recognize two basic truths. The first is that this salvation history is a process. The second is that this process of redemptive history finds its goal, its focus and fulfilment in the person and work of Christ. This is the principle underlying this book.

Failure to grasp this truth – largely because the proper study of the Old Testament has been neglected, has aided and abetted one of the most unfortunate reversals in evangelical theology. The core of the gospel, the historical facts of what God did in Christ, is often *down-graded* today in favour of a more mystical emphasis on the private spiritual experience of the individual. Whereas faith in the gospel is essentially acceptance of, and commitment to, the declaration that God acted in Christ some two thousand years ago on our behalf, saving faith is often portrayed nowadays more as trust in what God is doing in us now. Biblical ideas such as 'the forgiveness of sins' or 'salvation' are interpreted as primarily describing a Christian's personal experience. But when we allow the whole Bible – Old and New Testaments – to speak to us, we find that those subjective aspects of the Christian life which are undoubtedly important – the new birth, faith and sanctification – are the *fruits* of the gospel. This gospel, while still relating to individual people at their point of need, is rooted and grounded in the history of redemption. It is the good news *about* Jesus, before it can become good news for sinful men and women. Indeed, it is only as the *objective* (redemptive-historical) facts are grasped that the *subjective* experience of the individual Christian can be understood.

At this point, some readers may be thinking that we have strayed from our original aim by discussing the history of biblical interpretation. I hope that a few technical points will not deter them, for it is my solid conviction that all Christians need to develop a biblical way of understanding the Bible and of using it. It is not only possible but even necessary for all Christians, including children, to gain a total perspective on the whole Bible so that the really important relationships between its parts begin to appear.

CHAPTER TWO

Bridging the Gap

THE FIRST GAP WE MUST BRIDGE IS THE GAP OF TIME AND CULTURE. The people and events of the Bible are so far away from us. In fact, the more we become aware of the historical context of any portion of the Bible, the more we come to recognize the great gap in time, language and thought forms which separates us from that text.

But time and culture are not the only aspects of that gap. There is a more vital dimension to the Bible which has to do with how God has revealed himself as well as *what* he has revealed a dimension which is bound up with what we call 'theology'. Perhaps it should be said right now that the word *theology* properly refers to the knowledge of God, that is, to what is to be known about God through his self-revelation. Only in a secondary way can the word be applied to the whole variety of religious study and discussion carried on both by people who accept God's self-revelation in Scripture and people who disagree with (parts of) it. We look at this in greater detail at the end of Chapter 3.

A STRAIGHTFORWARD EXAMPLE

To illustrate the problem of this gap of time, culture and theology, let us suppose that we, as contemporary Christians, open our Bible at one of Paul's letters. We read some of his theological exposition and then move on to the exhortation to live consistently with the truths of the gospel. Granting that certain adjustments have to be made, certain allowances for the fact that Paul wrote nineteen hundred years ago to some people in Asia Minor or Italy, we nevertheless do not feel that this is a serious barrier to our understanding. More important, we do not find that this gap seriously inhibits us from accepting Paul's words to, say, the Galatians as God's word to us. The reason is obvious: Paul addressed a group of Christians on the basis of the gospel and we recognize that, despite the difference in time and culture, there is sufficient common ground theologically between the first and the twentieth centuries for us to hear the words as if addressed to us.

As we analyse what has been happening, we see that we have recognized almost intuitively that, from the point of view of God's revelation and God's dealings with men, the Christian church in all ages is one. It belongs to the same era of God's dealings. The limits of this era at one end are the birth of the New Testament church at Pentecost, and at the other the return of Christ in power and glory to judge the living and the dead. Whenever we come to a text outside these bounds, the gap is widened, and greater care and skill is required to bridge it.

THE 'GAP' WIDENS

Let us take a short step back from our clearly defined 'gospel' era. In Acts 1 Luke describes a situation – the post-resurrection appearances and ascension of Jesus – that is dramatically different from ours in that it occurs before the giving of the Holy Spirit. There is a uniqueness about this period, also shared by the Pentecost narrative in Acts 2, which raises the question how much can such a unique period provide information which applies directly to us? After all, we do not share the situation of the people as they waited for the once-for-all beginning of a new era. An important principle of biblical interpretation is involved that we must not generalize the events of a historical narrative without some good reason for doing so. (What makes a good reason is a question we shall examine later.)

In the same way we may continue to move further into biblical history increasing our distance from the normal Christian situation to which we belong. The Gospels, for example, contain much narrative dealing with a time which is not only pre-Pentecost, but also pre-Resurrection and pre-Crucifixion. We may not simply assume that narrative about disciples and their relationship to Jesus in his earthly life provides normative instruction for us. We know that we have to make adjustments for the fact that our relationship with Jesus, who is not here in the flesh but in heaven, is by faith and through his Spirit dwelling in us. We now look back on the finished work of Christ in his life, death and resurrection, while the narratives of the Gospels only anticipate this completion. It may be, for example, that John 1: 12 does have relevance to modern evangelism – '*to all who received him, who believed in his name, he gave power to become children of God*' – but we may not assume this until we have examined the original significance of the passage. It speaks of Jesus coming physically and literally to the Jews as their Messiah, he came to his own people, but they would not receive him (verse 11). The Jews as a whole did not acknowledge him as the Christ, but those who did were made children of God.

If we find this problem faces us even in the New Testament, we find much greater difficulty in the Old Testament. For there we are not only in a pre-Resurrection situation; we are in a pre-Incarnation and pre-Christian one. In fact the differences between the Old Testament situation and our own are much easier to discern than the similarities. Because of this we tend to grasp at the obvious similarities, so that they become our guide for interpretation and application. The God of Israel is our God and his character is unchanging. The faithful people of Israel, the 'saints' of the Old Testament, are true saints even though they do not know Christ. We tend to shelve the question of how they were saved without knowing Christ and simply ask instead how they illustrate the life of faith.

THE 'CHARACTER STUDY' APPROACH

It is here that the Old Testament character studies come into their own. There are many more real-life situations to draw from in the Old Testament than in the New – many more historical narratives that reveal to us men and women who are realistically portrayed, 'warts and all', in their encounters with God. But the difficulties we met in the historical narratives of the Gospels and Acts are increased when we come to the Old Testament narratives. We cannot simply transfer the experiences of the past wholesale to today. There are two dangers to avoid in regard to historical narrative:

(a) We must not view these recorded events as if they were a mere succession of events from which we draw little moral lessons or examples for life. Much that passes for application of the Old Testament text to the Christian life is only moralizing. It consists almost exclusively in *observing* the behaviour of the godly and the godless (admittedly against a background of the activity of God) and then *exhorting* people to learn from these observations. That is why the 'character study' is a favoured approach to Bible narrative – the life of Moses, the life of David, the life of Elijah and so on. There is nothing wrong with character studies as such – we are to learn by others' examples – but such character studies all too often take the place of more fundamental aspects of biblical teaching. Paradoxically, they may even lead us away from the basic foundations of the gospel. Certainly we do not solve the problem by using the allegorical method and turning every historical detail into a prefiguring of Christ without regard to the whole structure of the Bible.

(b) We must guard against a too-ready acceptance of the example of biblical characters, whether good or bad, as the source of principles of the Christian life. If we concentrate on how David saved Israel from Goliath, on what response Elijah made to the threats of Jezebel, on where Saul showed the chinks in his moral armour, as examples to follow or to avoid, then we have reduced the significance of these people to the lowest common denominator. This approach easily obscures any other unique characteristics that may be part of revelation.

The danger in the 'character study' approach is that it so easily leads to the use of the Old Testament characters and events as mere illustrations of New Testament truths, while at the same time giving the appearance of being a correct exposition of the meaning of the Word of God. But if the real substance is drawn from the New Testament, and it alone, we may well ask what is the point of applying ourselves to the Old Testament; why we may not just as well use non-biblical material to illustrate the New Testament. To make this criticism is not to deny the value of Old Testament narrative in illustrating New Testament principles; but we should not assume that such an approach uncovers the primary meaning of the text.

To press this point even further – it should be recognized that the 'character study' approach is frequently used in a way that implies quite wrongly that the reader today may identify with the character in question. But we must reckon with both the historical and theological uniqueness of the characters and events if we are not to misapply them. Is it in fact true that if God took care of baby Moses, God will take care of me? Such application simply assumes that what applied to the unique figure of Moses in a unique situation applies to all of us, and presumably all the time. But why should our children be privileged to identify with Moses rather than with other Hebrew children at the time who may not have escaped Pharaoh's wrath? The theological significance of Moses and of his preservation is all but ignored in this case.

With whom may the Christian identify in the narrative of David and Goliath – with the soldiers of Israel or with David? (Certainly not with Goliath!) But, someone will say, there is a lesson for us in both the soldiers and in David. The former show us the Christian who lacks faith, and the latter exemplifies the man who truly trusts God and overcomes against great odds (never mind the ingenious bit with the stones!). To a point this is true; the soldiers are afraid and David is a man who trusts God. But is that all? It certainly is not all when we read the narrative in its context, for then we find that there is something unique about David which cannot apply to us. David is the one who, immediately prior to the Goliath episode (I Samuel 17), is shown to be God's anointed king. He receives the Spirit of God to do mighty deeds for the saving of Israel, according to the pattern of saviours already established in the book of Judges. So when it comes to his slaying of Goliath it is as the unique anointed one of God that he wins the battle.

The application of this truth to the believer is somewhat different from a simple identification of the believer with David. Rather we should identify with the ordinary people of God, the soldiers, who stand and watch the battle fought on their behalf. The same point may be made about the lives of all the biblical characters who have some distinct office bestowed on them by God. If their achievement is that of any godly man the lesson is clear, but if it is the achievement of a prophet, a judge or the messianic king, then to that extent it no more applies to the people of God in general than does the unique work of Jesus as the Christ.

THE UNITY OF THE BIBLE

I have sought to put the problem as it is likely to confront us in the practical situations of Christian service – beach mission talks, Sunday School lessons and the like. The case of the anniversary speaker in the introduction is almost autobiographical. I'm sure such examples of misapplication still flourish. Behind it all is the problem of the unity of the Bible. This is not an academic question, but one in which even our children are involved at the simplest level of Bible instruction.

If we are to avoid flights of fancy in interpretation we need some understanding of what governs the right approach to the meaning of the Bible. Most of us assume (rightly, I believe) that there is some very basic unity to the whole Bible and to its message. It is more than a collection of holy books in that it contains a single story of salvation. If there is such a unifying theme throughout the Bible, then the *structure* of the biblical message – the overall relationship of each part to the whole – becomes of prime importance for interpretation.

We cannot escape the fact that every attempt to read the Bible is an exercise in the science of interpretation or, as it is called in technical terms, *hermeneutics*. Even a personal letter from a friend demands that you interpret the way your friend uses language to convey to you his intended meaning. We all know how much harder it is to converse by letter than by speaking face-to-face. In conversation we use not only words but also facial expressions and changes in the tone of voice. We can vary the speed, loudness, and the emphasis of words. We can stop and clarify a statement when a slight change in facial expression in our hearer signals lack of understanding. But the written word lacks many of these aids to interpretation even in a personal communication from someone we know well. Hermeneutics obviously cannot be ignored when we are dealing with the ancient texts of the Bible, for they were written in foreign languages and addressed to people of another age.

Let us use the analogy of a map. If you open a map or consult a tourist plan of a large city, one of the things you take for granted is that the plan represents a real unity. Thus we believe that the information on how to get from one place to another is based on the actual relationships of the parts of the city and of the streets which connect them. If someone, for a joke, had glued half a map of Sydney onto half a map of Melbourne, a planned journey from the Melbourne Town Hall to the Sydney Opera House would be impossible on the basis of that map. The two parts do not belong together and there is no unity. Now if we wish to move from a biblical text of the pre-Christian era to ourselves in the twentieth century of the gospel era, we must not only assume that there is a connection between the two, but we must understand how they connect. As with our map, so with the Bible – we must know the kind of unity that exists within it. Obviously this unity is not a static uniformity, as if the Bible were merely a large reservoir of proof texts which may be selected and applied at random with no thought for their context. Unfortunately some people tend to work with the

Bible on this basis with little credit to themselves or to the message they extract.

Let us think of this question of relationships in another way. There is a well-used saying: 'A text without a context is a pretext.' This sound wisdom reminds us that the Bible is not a collection of isolated sentences or verses to be used at random in establishing doctrine. One of the unhappy results of the division of the Bible into chapters and verses (which did not take place until the late Middle Ages) is an unnatural fragmenting of the text. Paul wrote one letter to the Romans, not sixteen separate chapters containing a varying number of units called verses. Most of us recognize this fact to a point – we know that anyone can prove almost anything by lifting a few verses out of context. We recognize also that the basic literary unit for conveying thought is the sentence. But do we always understand how much the meaning of a sentence is governed by its place in a larger unit of communication?

How wide must we stretch the context in order to gain a good understanding of one sentence? We might arbitrarily set a paragraph as the limit – if we could only be sure what the equivalent of a paragraph would be in the Hebrew or Greek text, which used neither paragraphs nor punctuation. But a paragraph usually occurs in the context of a number of other paragraphs. We could go from paragraphs to chapters (also units unknown to the authors), and then to the complete books. It may not always be necessary to go this far in providing the context needed for the understanding of a given verse or sentence, but any supposition of unity in the given book means that knowledge of the whole and knowledge of the parts are inseparable. The logical conclusion to be drawn is that, if the unity of the Bible has any meaning at all, the real context of any Bible text is the whole Bible. Any given text is more meaningful when related not only to its immediate context, but also to the entire plan of redemption revealed in the whole Bible.

SUMMARY

To summarize our problem: accepting the whole Bible as the Word of God raises the question of how it speaks to us in the twentieth century. How may we legitimately understand, as a relevant and living word from God, that which was addressed to people in situations of varying degrees of remoteness from our own?

To be aware of the nature of a problem is to be on the way to a solution. Our problem of interpretation is very closely bound up with the question of the nature of the unity of the Bible. We need to understand the relationships between the various parts of the Bible, and this means understanding not only the unity but also the disunity which is there. We have seen how the gap between us and the biblical text widens as we move farther back away from the gospel age to which we belong. The coming of Jesus in the flesh is the unique event which creates discontinuity in the Bible, and which has made its mark in human history through the distinction between B.C. and A.D.

We have seen some important differences between the post-Pentecost, the pre-Pentecost and the pre-Christian ages. We must now ask what unites these ages so that the sixty-six books of the Bible form an organic unity of revelation.

CHAPTER THREE

What is the Old Testament?

WHEN DEALING WITH ANYTHING AS COMPLEX AS THE OLD TESTAMENT
it is as well not to assume anything, but rather to attempt to
understand what makes up the complexity. (Readers who are
already fairly familiar with the Old Testament will need to be
patient at this point!)

The first and most obvious dimension of the Old Testament is the
literary one. The Old Testament is a book, or rather, a collection of
books. Secondly we note that a common feature of these books is
their association with a *history* which embraces a single continuous
time span and also a single continuous part of human history.
Thirdly, the Old Testament presents a *theological* dimension in that
the history, which is the subject of the literature, is represented as a
single history of God's dealings with the world and with man. Let
us now consider some of the implications of these three key
dimensions of the Old Testament (and for that matter of the whole
Bible) – the literary, the historical and the theological.

THE OLD TESTAMENT AS LITERATURE

The Old Testament is a collection of thirty-nine books written by a
variety of authors over a period of maybe 1,000 years or more.
Nearly all of the Old Testament was written in Hebrew, an ancient
language of the North-West Semitic group, which was closely
related to the language of the Canaanites. Some parts of the Old
Testament were written in Aramaic, another Semitic language
which was spoken throughout the Babylonian empire from where it
was adopted by the Jews in the sixth century B.C. The earlier parts
go back to the time of Moses, which was probably the thirteenth

century B.C., while the latest sections were written before the Greek period of the fourth century B.C.[1]

It has been customary to divide the individual books of the Old Testament into four groups: law, history, prophecy, and poetry. This has some value, but the classifications are very broad and it is helpful to be a little more specific about the literary types of the Bible. Different literary forms or types function in different ways and some appreciation of the various forms in Hebrew literature is essential if we are to avoid a misinterpretation of the authors' intentions. We must not expect the Hebrew authors to be bound by the same rules of literary expression to which we are accustomed. The Bible is not a bound volume of twentieth century works; it is an ancient collection using an ancient language to express thought forms which frequently differ from our own.

We should not be concerned to classify entire books since within any one book many different literary types may be found. Each type must be recognized for what it is before it can be properly interpreted. Thus the intention behind a section of historical narrative will be different from that which is behind a parable or a precept of the Mosaic Law. Some of the literary types will be familiar enough to us and will present few difficulties as literary expressions. Others will be strange to us, and their intention will be not so clear until we have discovered the nature and function of such types. In the Old Testament we find:

historical narratives	wisdom sayings of the
laws and statutes	proverbial kind
prophetic oracles	instructional wisdom
genealogies	hymns of praise
songs of many kinds	thanksgivings
taunts	laments
parables and fables	apocalytic visions . . .
riddles	and much else.

We do not have to become experts in ancient literary types in

---

[1] Scholarly opinion differs over the date of the Book of Daniel. Taken on face value, Daniel belongs to the sixth century B.C. and the book provides an account of events which occurred during the captivity in Babylon. Many modern scholars believe that Daniel is an exposition of the persecution of the Jews under the second century B.C. Hellenistic ruler Antiochus Epiphanes, and that it is cast into its sixth century mould in order to obscure to all but the initiated the true significance of the book.

order to avoid the pitfalls. But we should at least try to become more familiar with them and to understand the way they function. It is really amazing how neglected the literary dimension has become when you reflect that we are talking about the medium of communication used by God. It is equally amazing that some interpreters seek to impose a single code of interpretation of literature, such as 'literal' interpretation. Literalism is, of course, perfectly valid as an approach to literature, if it is conceived of broadly enough to accommodate the different ways in which language may be used to communicate. But it is not the purpose of this book to discuss the complex questions of literary types. Let us, however, maintain an openness to the ancient conventions of the literary medium of communication by becoming sensitive to the wonderful variety of expression in the Bible.

THE OLD TESTAMENT AS HISTORY

We cannot hope to understand the way the Old Testament functions as part of the Bible, without some grasp of the whole sweep of Old Testament history But the answer, for most of us, is not to wade through a large volume on the history of Israel. That should come later. We ought to begin with a basic frame-work of biblical history, a 'birds-eye view', which will show us the main events in the progression of the history. This, contrary to supposition, is easily done for there is really a very simple historical outline to be discerned in the Bible, even if this is not the immediate impression gained by the reader who has become bogged down in the Books of Kings. The simple diagram on page 33, which I learned from one of my own teachers, provides one effective representation of the history in the Old Testament.

The simplicity of this diagram allows for further detail to be added as one becomes more familiar with the contents of the Old Testament. It cannot be over-emphasized that, without a sense of the historical progression and of the relationship between the principal events and characters, it would be very difficult to make much sense out of the Bible. The overwhelming conviction of the biblical authors is of the activity of God in history. God acts not in a fragmentary, capricious or unrelated way, but in a single purposeful span of history. The Bible is not a deposit of abstract ideas or even of formulated doctrines, but a marvellous unity of salvation-history.

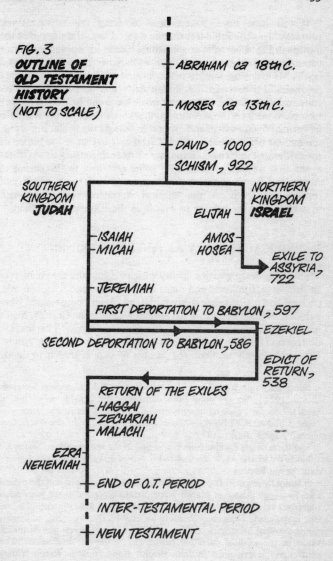

FIG. 3
OUTLINE OF OLD TESTAMENT HISTORY
(NOT TO SCALE)

ABRAHAM ca 18th C.

MOSES ca 13th C.

DAVID, 1000

SCHISM, 922

SOUTHERN KINGDOM **JUDAH**

NORTHERN KINGDOM **ISRAEL**

ELIJAH

ISAIAH
MICAH

AMOS
HOSEA

EXILE TO ASSYRIA, 722

JEREMIAH

FIRST DEPORTATION TO BABYLON, 597

EZEKIEL

SECOND DEPORTATION TO BABYLON, 586

EDICT OF RETURN, 538

RETURN OF THE EXILES

HAGGAI
ZECHARIAH
MALACHI

EZRA
NEHEMIAH

END OF O.T. PERIOD

INTER-TESTAMENTAL PERIOD

NEW TESTAMENT

If you have never taken time to grasp the basic historic progression of the Bible it is time to do so. I would suggest that the outline in Fig. 3 be used, or something like it, in conjunction with a summary of biblical history such as can be found in numerous books.[2] It may be helpful to point out that it is sometimes necessary to distinguish between the Bible's historical schema and the reconstructions of biblical history made by some historians. Many historians work on the assumption that we can accept only what can be verified from sources and evidences outside the Bible. For some, the earliest biblical history that is verifiable is that of the period of the settlement in Canaan in the late thirteenth century B.C.[3] Others assert that we can go back with some certainty to the period of Abraham.[4] But here we are not concerned with the possibility of testing the truth of the biblical narrative, but only with understanding the pattern of events as the Bible presents them.

BIBLICAL HISTORY AS THE BIBLE PRESENTS IT

We are thus dealing with a history which begins with the creation of the universe, the world and man. The history then focuses on man (Adam) and on his relationship with God. After being ejected from paradise in Eden because of his rebellion against the Creator, man's history is one of increasing and widespread sinfulness. This leads to destruction through the flood and to the preservation of one family. From this family of Noah the lineage of man is shown to divide

[2] For example see John Stott, *Understanding the Bible* (London: Scripture Union, 1972); also any good Bible dictionary will provide an outline of biblical history. Fuller treatments can be found in John Bright, *History of Israel* (London: SCM Press, 1972) or Charles Pfeiffer, *Old Testament History* (Grand Rapids: Baker, 1979).

[3] The dates of the Exodus from Egypt and of the settlement in Canaan are subjects of debate. Most scholars today accept an early thirteenth century date for the Exodus.

[4] A major difference of opinion exists between John Bright and the radical Old Testament historian Martin Noth. Bright accepts that the patriarchal narratives ring true to the historical evidence in the kind of cultural world that is depicted. Thus on probability we may accept, according to Bright, the substantial historicity of these narratives. Noth rejects any historical value in the biblical narrative before the settlement in Canaan. The controversy is explained in John Bright, *Early Israel in Recent History Writing* (London, SCM Press, 1956).

among the nations of the world although the focus is on the line of Shem leading to Abraham.

Abraham was called by God to leave Mesopotamia and to go to Canaan where he received certain promises concerning his descendants (of which there were none as yet). This promise was later passed on to his son Isaac and to Isaac's son, Jacob. Eventually the descendants of Jacob migrated to Egypt and in time became a large nation. When this people was subjected to a cruel slavery by the Egyptians, God sent Moses to lead them into the land of Canaan which he had promised to give to Abraham's descendants. This process was long and involved and included the making of a covenant at Mount Sinai in which this nation of Israel was bound to God as his people with all that that implied.

The dispossession of the inhabitants of Canaan, and the settlement in the land, led to the development of the need for some form of government or administration of the covenant. After a false start under King Saul, Israel received a great leader in the person of David. He united the tribes, established a capital city, secured the borders and set up a proper administration. Unfortunately David's successor, Solomon, became too ambitious and unwise policies led to eventual dissatisfaction. When his son came to the throne, there was a rebellion and the ten tribes of the north seceded to become the kingdom of Israel while the dynasty of David continued to rule over the southern kingdom of Judah.

The secession led to a general decline in both north and south, although the prophets continued to call the people back to faithfulness to the covenant God. The north finally suffered defeat at the hands of the Assyrians (722 B.C.) and ceased to be an independent state. More than a century later the might of Babylon was aimed at the south and, with the destruction of Jerusalem (586 B.C.) and the deportation of most of the people, Judah as a political entity ceased to be.

The exile in Babylon came to an end for the Jews when Cyrus the Persian overcame the power of Babylon and allowed captive peoples to return home (538 B.C.). Many of the Jews chose to remain in Babylon, for life had been quite kind to them. But those who returned had a real struggle to reconstruct the state of Judah. Eventually, with Persian co-operation, some stability was reached and Jerusalem and the Temple were reconstructed. But the glory of the golden age of David and Solomon never returned and the Old Testament period comes to an end with a whimper rather than a bang!

Some three-and-a-half centuries intervened between the two Testaments. During this time the most complex political developments occurred in the Jewish state. The Persian Empire crumbled when Alexander the Great pushed into Asia Minor and advanced to Egypt and beyond Babylon to the borders of India. Hellenistic culture was imposed upon Alexander's empire by his successors and the Jews did not escape the fearful results of the conflict between the pagan Greek philosophies and way of life, and the Hebrew devotion to the Law and religion of the one True God. In the middle of the first century B.C., the Romans entered the Middle East region and the Jews found themselves a province of the great Roman Empire.

WHAT OLD TESTAMENT HISTORY IS NOT

At first sight the history contained in the Old Testament may seem to be that of a fairly insignificant nation, which spent most of its time in political subjection to whatever great power had the ascendancy in the Middle East. Unfortunately this is often the impression to be gained from a concentration on the details of Old Testament history. Now, the study of detail is certainly important but it is a human weakness to fail 'to see the wood for the trees'. Too much initial concentration on the details of Israel's history may obscure important relationships and the overall pattern in the events.

It is essential to remember one of the cardinal points of history writing, – that no history is ever the mere record of a succession of details or events. The historian writes *selectively* according to his *purpose*. Of course he cannot completely isolate one aspect of human life from all others, but he can direct his attention to one or other aspect so that others fall more or less into the background. Thus we might have in relation to the same nation in the same period of time a political history, an economic history, a social history, a military history and so on.

What kind of history is Old Testament history? First let us see what it is not. It is not merely a history of *Israel*, for part of it deals with a period before the birth of the nation, and this material cannot be treated as only background. Genesis I–II is far too important to be dismissed so simply.

Nor is Old Testament history a *religious* history, for that would entail nothing more than the attempts of historians to deal with religious thought and activity. The Old Testament claims to be much more than that, especially since it continually passes judgement upon mankind's religious activity – even upon that of the Israelites. In fact, to treat the Bible as a history of religions was the great mistake of the rationalistic age of the nineteenth century.

WHAT OLD TESTAMENT HISTORY IS

Insofar as the Old Testament is history, it is a *theological* history. Rather than a religious history (a human record of human religion), it is God's record of God's own dealings with the world and with men. It is characteristic of the Bible that it does not record the events in the affairs of men as if they were determined by chance, by blind fate, or by a necessary chain of prior events. The history of the Bible is *purposive*; the purpose which governs the events is God's purpose. The biblical historians relate events, not as events in themselves, but as the deed of God – or as the deeds of men which are to be judged according to the character of God. It is God who calls Abraham from Ur, who brings Israel out of Egypt, who raises up Cyrus to free Israel from Babylon, and who judges human actions according to whether they are good or bad in his sight. It is this purposive element in biblical history which makes the Bible unique, giving it its distinctive dimension.

Furthermore the biblical history (history-as-the-Bible-presents-it, rather than merely the history of Bible times) is therefore a part of God's word to man. God's own interpretation of the events of biblical history makes known to us the purposes he is pursuing within this history. It is this interpretation of the events as God's events which give the Bible its character of divine revelation. This is the consistent testimony of the Bible as it records how God speaks to man *declaring* his purposes and intentions, how he acts on the basis of his word, and how he then *interprets* the events by his word. Thus we see, contrary to some modern interpretations, that God declares to Moses what he will do for Israel (free them from Egypt and give them Canaan) and on what basis he will do it (the promises to Abraham). When the Exodus has taken place, God then declares: 'I am the Lord your God who brought you out of the land of Egypt, out of the house of bondage' (Exodus 20: 2).

Now this purposive history not only reveals the mind of God; it also affects the way in which those thoughts are communicated. The selection of events and the recording of details is governed by the theological meaning rather than by any military or political significance. The theology controls the writing of the history. The fact that God acts in the history of men and interprets his acts means that these historical events will form a pattern that relates to the purposes of God. Biblical history is theological history.

WHAT IS THEOLOGY?

Theology means the knowledge of God as God himself reveals it. We have seen that biblical theology consists of the study of the revelation of God as he acts in this world, in the history of men. The most important concern in the study of the Bible is the revelation of God: What is God saying to us in the record of his acts? What did God do in entering in a special way into the history of mankind? We have already raised the question of the unity of the Bible; we are here asserting that the aspect which above all else creates the Bible's unity is its theology. It is the one God who acts and speaks throughout the history in the Bible. Furthermore God acts and speaks with a unity of purpose. God's message to us is one unified discourse, not a series of isolated and disconnected messages.

The task which lies ahead of us is to try to discern what God is saying and how he says it. In doing this we may say that we are primarily interested in revelation – in theology. But we may not separate what God says and does from the context in which he says it and does it (the history) nor from the way he says what he does (the literary record). We shall be looking for the essential unity of the Bible, without ignoring its diversity and its complexity.

CHAPTER FOUR

Biblical Theology and
the History of Redemption

THREE CHARACTERISTICS HAVE NOW BEEN PRESENTED IN OUR SEARCH
for unity and structure in the Bible. These are the literary forms,
the historical framework and the theological structures. Each must
be given its due weight and be taken into account in the process of
interpreting the biblical text. Since the really unique feature of the
Bible is its revelation of God and of his purposes (its theology), it is
unfortunate that so little emphasis is given these days to the study of
biblical theology. In recent years there have appeared numbers of
books, written at the non-academic level for the ordinary Christian
reader, which deal with surveys of the Bible as literature, with
biblical history and with Christian doctrine. But there is hardly a
book to be found on the subject of biblical theology.

CHRISTIAN DOCTRINE AND BIBLICAL THEOLOGY

We need to be aware of the distinction between Christian doctrine
and biblical theology. The approach to biblical interpretation
adopted in this book is based on the method of biblical theology.
Christian doctrine (systematic or dogmatic theology) involves a
systematic gathering of the doctrines of the Bible under various
topics to form a body of definitive Christian teaching about man,
sin, grace, the church, sacraments, ministry, and so on. This
systematizing of theology depends for its validity on the interpretation problem being satisfactorily handled. It asserts, on the basis
of the texts written *then*, what is the truth to be believed and
proclaimed *now*. However, it is important to see the limitations of
this approach. The structure and contents of the Bible are not
systematic – there is no one section which sets out the doctrine of

sin and another that of salvation. The formulation of Christian doctrine requires that we transform the material which is set within the framework of the dynamic processes of biblical history, into a form which is true to the Bible and applicable to the present time. The theologian wants to avoid the pitfalls of 'proof-texting' in which it is assumed that all biblical texts have equal value in establishing doctrine, irrespective of the context in which they occur. Thus the more static kind of propositions of Christian doctrine depend for their validity on the correct handling of the dynamic revelation which the Bible records in the very different form of an historical progression of God's dealing with man.

Biblical theology, as defined here, is dynamic not static. That is, it follows the movement and process of God's revelation in the Bible. It is closely related to systematic theology (the two are dependent upon one another), but there is a difference in emphasis. Biblical theology is not concerned to state the final doctrines which go to make up the content of Christian belief, but rather to describe the *process* by which revelation unfolds and moves toward the goal which is God's final revelation of his purposes in Jesus Christ. Biblical theology seeks to understand the relationships between the various eras in God's revealing activity recorded in the Bible. The systematic theologian is mainly interested in the finished article – the statement of Christian doctrine. The biblical theologian on the other hand is concerned rather with the progressive unfolding of truth. It is on the basis of biblical theology that the systematic theologian draws upon the pre-Pentecost texts of the Bible as part of the material from which *Christian* doctrine may be formulated.

Using the method of biblical theology we may examine how the events in the time of Moses, for example, relate theologically to the events predicted by the later prophets, and how these in turn relate to the New Testament gospel. If we can thus discern a development in the biblical revelation, we are in a better position to say what relevance the law of Moses, the narrative of the manna in the wilderness or any other event of the Old Testament, may have to us who live on the opposite side of the 'Christ event'.

THE HISTORY OF REDEMPTION AND THE KINGDOM OF GOD

We have seen that the Old Testament is not a mere textbook of the history of Israel as we understand it today, but a theological history.

How can we characterize this history so that we are able to see the real unity within it? I suggest we look at the Old Testament as a *history of redemption*. In other words, the key to the Old Testament is not the part Israel plays – as important as that is – but the part *God* plays in redeeming a people from slavery and making them his own. The first approach would be to reduce the Old Testament to an example of ancient national history; the second interprets Israel's history as a part of God's redeeming activity to man.

Nor is redemption the only theological idea which provides structure to the Old Testament, for redemption is a process which leads to a goal. Has not the Old Testament something to say about that goal? Indeed it has – the redeemed people of God are the people of God's kingdom. I would even suggest that this goal, *the Kingdom of God*, is a more central issue in the Old Testament than is the redemptive process of bringing people into that Kingdom. Of course we cannot really separate the two so strictly. The process needs a goal; the goal has to have a process or method of attainment.

SOME FEATURES OF THE HISTORY OF REDEMPTION

First the history of redemption is *progressive*. That is easy to see simply by comparing the light which the patriarchs (Abraham, Isaac and Jacob) had on God's purposes, with the understanding possessed by a post-exilic Jew who could draw on Moses and all the prophets. When we look at the New Testament, we find the full light of the gospel and all its implications are expounded. Central to this gospel is the Kingdom (see for example Mark 1: 14–15).

Does this mean that truth was rather dimly understood at the start, and became brighter until the coming of Jesus? Not really. The idea of a gradual 'dawning of the light' is useful to a point, but it does not explain what appear to be important peaks or climaxes within the process. What we find is a series of stages, each self-contained, each coming to a climax leading in turn to a new stage. The emphases given to certain events and people historically and theologically, direct the reader's attention to such climaxes.

Secondly the history of redemption is *incomplete without the New Testament*. The fact that the Kingdom forecast by the prophets is never fulfilled in the Old Testament is of concern only if we ignore the New Testament. The great 'saving events' of the Old Testament (the saving of Noah, the call of Abraham, the exodus from Egypt, the establishment of the united monarchy, the destruction of Jerusalem by Babylon and the prophetic forecast of the new and perfect kingdom) are all fulfilled in Christ and the Kingdom of Christ. It is the New Testament that gives focus to the saving events of the Old.

Christianity does not differ from Judaism by asserting that the Old Testament is incomplete, for Judaism also recognises the future hope of prophecy which remained unfulfilled in Old Testament times. Some, both Christians and Jews, have tended to lose sight of a future messianic fulfilment, and have thus reduced the Old Testament to a code of morals encased within an interesting but rather irrelevant era of ancient history. The essential difference between the two faiths lies in how the completion of the hope of Israel is brought about. According to the New Testament it is the Christ event which brings this hope to its appointed goal. Judaism, on the other hand, rejects Jesus of Nazareth as the awaited messianic fulfiller, and looks for other ways.

Thirdly the history of redemption is *to be interpreted*. Since our concern is with biblical theology first and foremost, we intend to follow the method which biblical theology requires:

(a) We begin with the New Testament because it is there that we encounter the Christ of the gospel, through whom by faith we are made God's children.

(b) The New Testament drives us back to the Old Testament because it everywhere presupposes the Old Testament as the basis of the gospel.

(c) The New Testament establishes for us that the Old Testament involves promise and hope of a goal which is fulfilled in Christ. It thus directs us to take account of 'the dynamic', the living process and movement, of the Old Testament which leads us on to the Christ of the Gospels. Because the New Testament declares the Old Testament to be incomplete without Christ we must understand the Old Testament in the light of its goal which is Christ. Jesus is indispensable to a true understanding of the Old Testament as well as the New.

APPLYING THE TEXT TO TODAY

All this is of interest because it opens the way to making the biblical text applicable to ourselves. Biblical theology shows us the kind of bridge needed to overcome the gap between the text and the

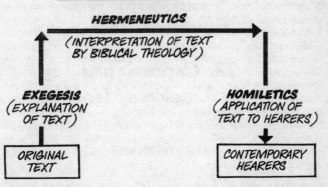

FIG. 4 **BRIDGING THE GAP BETWEEN TEXT AND HEARERS**

HERMENEUTICS
(INTERPRETATION OF TEXT BY BIBLICAL THEOLOGY)

EXEGESIS
(EXPLANATION OF TEXT)

HOMILETICS
(APPLICATION OF TEXT TO HEARERS)

ORIGINAL TEXT

CONTEMPORARY HEARERS

modern Christian. It may be helpful at this point to outline the three stages involved in bringing the text across to ourselves.

(*a*) *Exegesis*   This is the term used to refer to the business of finding out what the text originally meant. Before we can ever show the relevance of any part of the Bible we must know what its author intended to convey to his readers.

(*b*) *Hermeneutics*   The hermeneutic or interpretative process is concerned with showing how the ancient biblical text has general relevance here and now. This book is mainly concerned with this stage and seeks to show how interpretation depends on the structure of the revelation of the Bible.

(*c*) *Application*   The general application of the text is turned into specific application to the life of the reader or hearer. Homiletics (preaching) is one such method of application as the preacher brings the meaning of the text from its original meaning (exegesis) through its general Christian interpretation (hermeneutics) to its specific way of addressing the congregation.

CHAPTER FIVE

The Covenant and the Kingdom of God

THE COVENANT

THE CREATION OF MAN IN THE IMAGE OF GOD DISTINGUISHED MAN from the animals. Man is not the end of a chain of evolution for he is qualitatively distinct from the animals. Man was created in fellowship with God and with dominion over the rest of the created order. Thus there is a unique relationship between God and man. However, we cannot ignore the similarity between man and the animals – man is never more than a creature and, as such, totally dependent upon the Creator. For instance the word of God to Adam forbidding him to eat from the tree of the Knowledge of Good and Evil expresses the fact that man, the creature, is bound by the limits of his creaturehood. There are real limits set by the Creator. As such they are expressions of the sovereignty of God – of his absolute lordship. But this Lord is good and he establishes his creature-man in a relationship which brings both rule and blessing. God is king, man his subject. And the peace where all this happens is the very best place of all – it is the garden paradise of Eden.

The Heart of the Problem

Man's sin is his attempt to renounce his creaturehood and to assert his independence of God, the Creator. The consequent judgement (in the 'fall' of man) establishes a break in the relationship between man and God. The world becomes a fallen world for fallen man to live in (see Romans 8: 19–20). But just as a fallen creation still reflects God's glory (Psalm 19: 1, Romans 1: 20) so man still reflects something of God's image. One aspect of the mercy of God is that he reveals a gracious attitude towards fallen man. Even in the Fall,

God's grace permits the world to continue, and sustains an order in which man may live and multiply.

The measure of God's grace is not only the 'common grace' shown in the ongoing universe; it is seen in the declaration of the purpose to redeem a people to be the people of God. The relationship between God and man as it once existed in Eden provides some indication of God's intention for his new race of people.

The Covenant with Abraham

Leaving aside for the moment the question of what is revealed between the fall of man and the beginnings of the Hebrew nation (in Genesis 4–11), we now examine the call of Abraham. God's promise to Abraham, expressed in Genesis 12 and subsequent chapters, provides one of the central themes of the Bible. The form of the promise described as *covenant* is essentially an agreement between parties. But this is no ordinary human covenant involving mutual consent of equals, but a lordly covenant dispensed by the gracious act of a God greatly offended and sinned against. The covenant is an agreement in the sense that the recipient must agree to any terms that may be proposed. But before all else we must see this covenant as one of *grace* – undeserved favour. God's promises to Abraham involved:

(a) a people who are his descendants,

(b) a land in which they will live,

(c) a relationship with God in that they shall be God's people.

This covenant relationship, then, consists in being called the people of God. Every later expression of this relationship stems from the original covenant. We discover that this promise to the forefathers of Israel (Abraham, Isaac and Jacob) becomes the basis of the relationship of all the people of God in the Bible. Even in the New Testament the concept of being the children of Abraham is transferred to those who by faith embrace the gospel (Galatians 3: 29). Every Christian is a son or daughter of Abraham! Later we shall look at the different areas where the covenant is given distinct expression in the Old Testament.

THE KINGDOM OF GOD

To understand the covenant we must examine its contents and its terms. The content of the covenant, like the goal of redemption, is the Kingdom of God, since the covenant is related to our redemption as children of God. What is the Kingdom of God? The New Testament has a great deal to say about 'the Kingdom' but we may best understand this concept in terms of the relationship of ruler to subjects. That is, there is a king who *rules*, a people who are *ruled*, and a sphere where this rule is *recognized* as taking place. Put in another way, the Kingdom of God involves:

(a) God's people
(b) in God's place
(c) under God's rule.

Given this basic analysis, it is clear that the fact that the term 'Kingdom of God' does not occur in the Old Testament is unimportant. The basic idea is woven through the whole of Scripture.

We first see the Kingdom of God in the Garden of Eden. Here Adam and Eve live in willing obedience to the word of God and to God's rule. In this setting, the Kingdom is destroyed by the sin of man – and the rest of the Bible is about the restoration of a people to be the willing subjects of the perfect rule of God.

There are many more episodes in the Bible where the Kingdom of God is given expression.

The Promise to Abraham

This is recorded in Genesis 12. 1–3. God promises the patriarchs that their descendants (God's people) will possess the promised land (God's place) and be the people of God, underneath his authority (God's rule). The historical process by which the people are brought into that situation takes the form of a redemptive act of God. God redeems Israel when he rescues it out of captivity in Egypt.

The Monarchy

Israel's 'golden age' comes during the period of the Monarchy, when northern and southern kingdoms are united as one nation. The political, economic and religious achievement of the kingdom of David and Solomon fulfils in a very tangible way the promises to Abraham. This kingdom is by no means perfect but it displays all the elements of the Kingdom of God. So a pattern is emerging: the revelation of God's kingdom begins with a very basic promise to Abraham, and then moves through a process of fulfilment which includes a redemptive experience (the Exodus) and climaxes in a fulfilment (the Monarchy). This last stage contains some things not even specifically stated in the original promise (such as the city of Zion, the Temple and the Kingship of David).

The Prophetic Kingdom

Solomon's kingdom fails and this serves to underline what has been apparent all along – that the historical process from Abraham to Solomon always falls short of the glory of God's true kingdom, even though it reveals the nature of that kingdom. In the face of the judgement upon Israel's sin (climaxing in the destruction of the nation), the prophets restate the promise of the Kingdom as something that will be fulfilled in the future.

The return from the Babylonian exile fails to produce the Kingdom foretold by prophets such as Isaiah, Jeremiah and Ezekiel. The post-exilic prophets, Haggai, Zechariah and Malachi, continue to direct the eyes of Israel away from their present history to the great future day when the perfect and everlasting Kingdom of God will be revealed. The Old Testament ends on the note of promise and expectation. There is no fulfilment in sight as the Jews enter nearly four hundred years of prophetic silence between the two Testaments. During this time the Jews develop a variety of solutions to the problem. The best known is that of the Pharisees, who sought a literal return to the Israelite monarchy and the freedom of Israel from all foreign oppression.

The Gospel Kingdom

Jesus declares: 'The time is fulfilled; the Kingdom of God is at hand' (Mark 1: 14). He thus introduces the gospel as the bringing-near of the Kingdom. What it means for the Kingdom to be 'at hand' rather than fulfilled emerges as the New Testament expounds the gospel. Jesus is the fulfilment of the promises but, at this stage, the fact that God's kingdom will triumph can only be received by faith. The New Testament describes in various places the future consummation of the Kingdom where the people of God know fully and by sight that which they now only have by faith. When Christ appears at his second coming, the saints of God will appear with him and the eternal Kingdom will be made plain (Colossians 3: 4).

It is now clear why the history of redemption is not simply a gradual unfolding of the truths of the Kingdom, a dawning of the

FIG. 5 **"KINGDOM" REVELATION IN THE BIBLE**
    (see also FIG. 8)

THE KINGDOM-PATTERN   —— **EDEN**
            ESTABLISHED

—————————————————————————————————————

THE FALL

—————————————————————————————————————

                                    REDEMPTIVE ACT:
                                    NOAH

THE KINGDOM **PROMISED** —————— **ABRAHAM**
                                    REDEMPTIVE ACT:
                                    EXODUS

THE KINGDOM **FORESHADOWED** —— **DAVID - SOLOMON**
                                    REDEMPTIVE ACT:
                                    PROPHETIC PROMISE
                                    OF SALVATION

THE KINGDOM **AT HAND** ———— **JESUS CHRIST**
                                    REDEMPTIVE ACT:
                                    HIS LIFE, DEATH
                                    AND RESURRECTION

THE KINGDOM **CONSUMMATED** — **RETURN OF CHRIST**

light, but rather a series of stages in which the Kingdom, and the way into it, are revealed. In each stage all the essential ingredients of the Kingdom are given expression, but each successive stage builds on the former until the full revelation of the gospel is achieved. At the risk of over-simplification, we might organize our material on the Kingdom of God in several 'blocks' of revelation:

(a) The Kingdom revealed in Eden
(b) The Kingdom revealed in Israel's history (Abraham to Solomon)
(c) The Kingdom revealed in prophecy (Elijah to John the Baptist)
(d) The Kingdom revealed in Christ (New Testament times to return to Christ).

We must now consider in a more exact fashion just how these stages or blocks of revelation relate to each other. The conclusions we reach about this will control our method of interpreting Old Testament texts and our understanding of their relevance to us as Christians today.

CHAPTER SIX

The Kingdom Revealed in Eden

THE CREATION

THE CREATION STORY MUST NEVER BE REGARDED MERELY AS A SORT OF biblical 'once-upon-a-time'. The fact that God is Creator and that man is his creature establishes at the outset the basis for understanding the Kingdom of God. When we speak of the *sovereignty* of God, we use a word which means his kingship, a kingship which is absolute and uncompromised. The creature is ruled and belongs, as a creature, within the sphere of God's perfect rule. In making all things by the power of his word (II Peter 3: 5), God shows the right he has as Creator to rule all things. The only perfect existence for the creature is that which is found within the framework of the rule of God.

The creatorship of God tells us that all reality is *God's* reality; all truth is *God's* truth. Nothing exists except by the will and word of God. One could write whole books on the implication of creation for a Christian approach to education, politics, economics, family life, moral values, or scientific research. If we believe in God as Creator, we may not divide the world into spiritual and secular. The fact that all reality depends upon the creative word of God means that the word of God must judge the ideas of men about truth and error, not the other way round. Thus the Christian doctrine of the authority of Scripture has its roots in the Creation. The famous comment about the Bible's authority made by the nineteenth century preacher C. H. Spurgeon ('Defend the Bible? I'd as soon defend a lion!') is well-known and appropriate. But we also need to be reminded of the relationship of God's word to the reasoning of man the creature about what is true – one does not take a pocket flashlight and shine it on the sun to see if the sun is real![1] The truth of God's word cannot be subject to the puny light of man's self-centred reason. God's word created what is and must interpret what is.

MAN IN THE IMAGE OF GOD

What is 'our image' (Genesis 1: 26)? God created man in his image and delegated to man authority over the rest of the created order (Genesis 1: 26f). Some scholars see this dominion of man, his *ruling-function* in creation, as the 'image' of God. Others point out that man in the image of God is both male and female. The 'image' may therefore be seen in the *relationship of man and woman*, particularly that which comes to its fullest expression in the union of husband and wife and which is based upon their sexual polarity (Genesis 2: 24). If the Bible does not clearly define the image of God in man at this stage, it will later point to Jesus Christ as the true image of God.

The basic points to notice at this stage are (i) the uniqueness of man as the summit of creation and the image of God and (ii) the creaturehood of man who is wholly dependent upon the Creator for his existence.

EDEN – THE GARDEN KINGDOM

As Creation speaks to us of the King, so Eden speaks to us of the Kingdom of God. In the previous chapter we saw that the Kingdom of God (a New Testament term) is a wholly biblical idea – the concept of the Kingdom dominates the whole biblical story. The point where this pattern is established is the Garden of Eden. Here we see the people of God (Adam and Eve in their innocence), the garden paradise (the place which God prepared as the perfect environment for his people) and the rule of God expressed by his word. God, as the sovereign king, sets the limits of freedom: 'You may freely eat of every tree of the garden but of the tree of knowledge of good and evil you shall not eat' (Genesis 2: 16–17).

---

[1] This aspect of the proper function of human reason is discussed in C. van Til, *Apologetics*, (unpublished syllabus, Westminster Theological Seminary, Philadelphia (n.d.) p. 67).

Because this is the Kingdom the king may not be challenged by his subjects. The perfect relationship between Creator and creature, between ruler and ruled, cannot exist if the creature seeks to usurp the role of Creator by rejecting his rule: 'For in the day that you eat of it you shall die' (Genesis 2:17).

The description of the Garden of Eden does not tell us everything about the Kingdom of God, but it does provide the essential framework for understanding the nature of the Kingdom as:

> God's people (Adam and Eve)
> in God's place (the Garden of Eden)
> under God's rule (the word of God).

We shall see this pattern emerge over and over as the goal of all God's activity. As it was in the creation, so it will be in the redemptive process which leads to the new creation. It is not accidental that the tree of life, which was denied to rebellious Adam, turns up in the description of the new Jerusalem in Revelation 22 (compare Genesis 3: 22f with Revelation 22: 2) or in John's prophecy of the victory of the saints in Revelation 2: 7: 'To him who conquers I will grant to eat of the tree of life which is in the paradise of God.'

THE FALL OF MAN

As with the creation, so it is easy to underestimate the significance and effects of the Fall. If the creatorship of God is given its full weight, then the Fall, as the outcome of man's unilateral declaration of independence, is a very serious thing. The serpent's temptation was directed to this end: 'Has God said . . .?' This initially subtle questioning of the authoritative word of God is followed by the outright denial of the truth of that word: 'You will not die' (Genesis 3: 1–4). The result was that Adam and Eve rejected the rule of God and asserted that even in the activity of reasoning, they were quite self-sufficient and independent.

It is impossible for God to be true to himself and at the same time tolerate his own dethronement by the creature. Thus judgement is both inevitable and radical (in the sense of striking at the root of the situation). 'On the day that you eat of it you will die' said God, and die man did. The fact that the final physical sign of death in the dissolution of the body was not immediate did not lessen the fact of

death which came upon man. Dead man is sinful man, man who has
rejected the Kingdom of God. Dead man is man outside the
Garden.

The Sovereignty of God and the Kingdom of God

We need to distinguish here between the absolute sovereignty of
God and the Kingdom of God. Neither man nor devil can escape the
sovereign power of God, no matter how hard either may fight
against it. In the end all who rebel against the Creator will be forced
to submit to the undeniable reality of God's lordship. But the
Kingdom of God as the Bible reveals it is the sphere of God's rule in
which his creatures submit willingly to this righteous rule. God's
sovereign rule is universal; the Kingdom of God is not. There is hell
as well as heaven, the world of darkness as well as the Kingdom of
light.

At this stage it is not necessary to supplement the records of
Genesis with the New Testament material, which enlarges upon the
meaning of the sentence of death which came upon man at the Fall.
The Genesis account provides the framework upon which the
Scriptures elaborate. It is impossible to separate the seemingly
contradictory elements in the Fall of man – the righteous
judgement of God and the incredible graciousness of God.

Judgement

The judgement involves firstly the disruption of the relationship
between man and God. This is most clearly seen in the ejection of
man from the Garden. Secondly there is the disruption of the
relationship between man and woman, as the perfect harmony of
male and female gives way to rivalry and accusation (Genesis 3: 12,
16). Thirdly there is a disruption of the relationship of man to his
environment as the physical creation is no longer seen to be under
the dominion of man (Genesis 3: 17–19). The word 'disruption' is
not intended to detract from the seriousness of the sentence of
death. Man outside the Kingdom is not merely under the sentence
of death, but he is dead. The real meaning of death lies in the
separation of man from the willing relationship of the Kingdom.
Autonomous man is God-denying and therefore life-denying as
well. Fallen man is dead spiritually. Outside of Eden there is no

return. Man has made his choice to be a rebel and he is bound by his decision. Nor is there any free choice for the posterity of Adam. Adam's fall from the Garden Kingdom is a fall of the whole human race. Every man is born outside the garden; every man is born an active rebel asserting autonomy and independence of the God of life. Human history and Scripture will show that man's death state means that he infallibly chooses to hate God, for that is his 'outside-Eden' nature. It is no longer a question of freedom to choose right or wrong, for man is free now only to be what he is – a sinner who hates God (cf. Romans 3: 9–18, 8: 6–8). Man has become a slave to sin – a slavery that is death.

Grace

Grace refers to the attitude of God towards rebellious sinners in showing to them mercy which is not only undeserved, but the very opposite of what is deserved. This attitude of God is not an abstract thing, but is known to us only through the saving activity of God. The incredible story of Genesis 3 is one of both judgement and grace. To begin with, we note that God does not purpose to obliterate man as he might justly have done when Adam sinned. The very fact that the race is preserved and that God continues to speak to man is a mark of his grace.

Grace is seen in the judgement of the serpent. God is righteous, and the father of lies is destined for his ultimate reward. Genesis 3: 15 has long been recognized as a word of grace, a *proto-evangel* (that is, the first reference to the gospel), promising that the 'seed of woman' shall actually share in the reversal of wrong. The serpent has led man to his fall and is blameworthy. Man is also blameworthy because he was willingly led. Grace operates in the face of blameworthiness.

Grace is seen in the maintenance of some semblance of society. The image of God in man is not entirely obliterated and hence man retains some dignity over the rest of creation. Man and woman continue to relate and to propagate even though the relationship is corrupted. The universe, in order to remain under man's dominion, and despite its ongoing challenge to man's dominion, is made to fall with man. The world outside the garden is fallen, for man cannot survive in an unfallen world. 'The creation was subjected to futility, not of its own will but by the will of him who subjected it in hope' (Romans 8: 20).

THE TWO LINES OF MAN

Genesis 4–11 contains a compact story which covers a very long
period of time. In keeping with the method of biblical theology, we
look at the emphases of these chapters in order to discover the
overall message they contain. This first history of fallen man in a
fallen world is an example of history that is theologically orientated.
The two lines of people, characterized by the heads of the lines Cain
and Abel, the sons of Adam and Eve, are arranged schematically.
The device of genealogy, or family tree, is used a number of times in
the Bible and we should not be too quick to dismiss the genealogies
as uninteresting or spiritually irrelevant. The diagram below
demonstrates the genealogical structure of Genesis 4–11.

FIG. 6 THE TWO LINES OF MAN

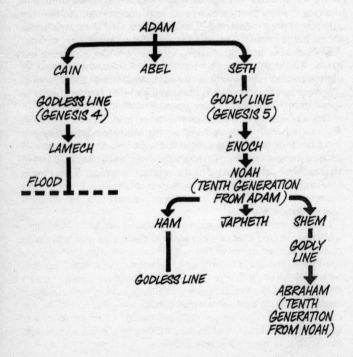

The narrative of Cain and Abel depicts one effect of the fall of mankind – rivalry and murder. The account then turns to the genealogy of Cain's ungodly line of descendants, characterized as developers of the city and of industry, and climaxed by the viciousness of Lamach (Genesis 4: 17–24). The godlessness of man is again stressed in Genesis 6 as God declares his intention to destroy man (v. 7). This godless line of course disappears in the flood.

Meanwhile a godly line begins with Seth who takes the place of his murdered brother (Genesis 4: 25). The exemplars of this line are Enoch, who walked with God, and Noah who found grace in the eyes of the Lord. The salvation of Noah and his family is an act of God's grace leading to a new beginning.

Again, however, there comes a division of mankind, with Ham as the principal representative of the godless. Shem is the father of the godly (Genesis 11: 10–26). We now have a godly line shown in a genealogy of ten generations from Adam to Noah, and ten generations from Noah to Abram. Clearly this is not haphazard. The story is moving towards a goal, and we shall have to examine the significance of Abram in order to find out where.

For the moment we may say that the foundations of redemption are being laid. Man the rebel, dead in his sins and wickedness (Ephesians 2:1), is the object of God's promise and grace. God's grace is shown in the saving of Noah and the continuation of a godly line. Already there is evidence of the relationship which God wants to have with a new race of men, and there are signs that the Kingdom of God will break into the fallen world in a demonstration of redemptive mercy. Man can dare to hope that once again he will see that Kingdom which is characterized by God's people in God's place under God's rule.

CHAPTER SEVEN

The Kingdom Revealed in Israel's History

WE HAVE SEEN HOW THE PATTERN FOR THE KINGDOM OF GOD is set in Eden. In this chapter we outline the structure of Israel's history from Abraham to the Babylonian Exile, a period of over a thousand years. We will not be concerned to summarize the historical facts (these can be found in any handbook or Bible dictionary), but rather to uncover the structure of the whole range of history – to see a purposeful relationship in the whole sequence of events. As Christians, we recognize that Israel's history is not haphazard, nor a series of random incidents, but, as in *all* history, it is governed by the purpose of God. The unique feature of Israel's history was that its purpose involved both revelation of salvation and the way of salvation. Since God is Lord, and since salvation has reference to the bringing of sinners into the Kingdom of God, that same Kingdom will be reflected in the history which is 'salvation history'.

ABRAHAM AND THE PATRIARCHS –
THE KINGDOM PROMISED

The most important thing about the history of Abraham is God's covenant promise. The whole narrative (Genesis 12–24) is dominated by the promises, which conveyed three main elements:

(a) Abraham's descendants would become a great nation (Genesis 12: 2, 13: 16, 15: 5, 16: 10, 18: 18).
(b) These descendants would possess the promised land (Genesis 12: 7, 13: 14–15, 15: 18–21, 17: 8).

(c) These descendants would be God's own people (Genesis 17: 2 and 7–8, 18: 19).

We should also note a fourth element which points to this gracious promise of God's being extended to those who are not physically descended from Abraham (see Genesis 12: 3. 17: 4–6, compare Romans 4: 16–18).[1]

What is this covenant promise if not the promise of the Kingdom of God? Certainly it is made in terms which are localized and earthbound. God in fact promises Abraham that his descendants would be God's people in God's place under God's rule, and all the Abraham stories must be seen in this light. An important element in the story is the way that tension develops because Abraham possesses the promise but not the substance of it. He must accept God at his word in faith, while at the same time all the natural events seem to work against the fulfilment of the promise. Even for Abraham the Kingdom of God must firstly be received by faith alone (Genesis 15: 6).[2]

Having been given promises of descendants and a land, Abraham watches his greedy nephew, Lot, occupy the best pasture land (Genesis 13: 8–11). But see how God then sustains Abraham with his promise (verses 14–17)![3] As for the promise of descendants, this is difficult for two very old people to accept (Genesis 15: 1–5) and the narrative of Hagar and Ishmael shows the stress Abraham and Sarah are under. Isaac, their natural-born son, is eventually designated the heir (Genesis 15: 4, 17: 19, 21, 18: 10). When Isaac is born the relief must have been enormous; he is truly the child of promise. So why the command to sacrifice the young boy (Genesis 22: 1–2)? This event shows that Abraham is not only obedient to God in a general way, but that he believes the specific promises of

[1] The multitude of nations has a double reference, for Abraham was the father of non-Israelite nations who did not directly share in the covenant, e.g. Ishmael's descendants and those of Esau (Edom). But the reference goes beyond this to the inclusion of the Gentiles in the blessings, as Paul indicates in Romans 4: 16–18.

[2] That is why Paul uses Genesis 15: 6 as the foundation for his exposition of the basic gospel truth that we are justified through faith (Romans 4).

[3] The difficult narrative in ch. 14 does not easily fit with the rest of this section in that it does not obviously express the same main emphases. However, the mysterious encounter with the priest king Melchizedek, and the paying of tithes to him, show that Abraham is content to forego the opportunity to enrich himself in this land until the land is his.

God, despite the apparent challenge to their fulfilment that the sacrifice would entail. Again he is reassured by the promise when his faith has stood firm (verses 15–18). When Sarah dies, Abraham is forced to haggle over the price of her burial plot which he must buy from his own inheritance (Genesis 23)!

Isaac's children, Esau and Jacob, are the objects of the sovereign choice of God, for the younger (again an unnatural choice) is selected over the elder for the covenant line (Genesis 25: 19–23). Jacob is not a good person at all – quite the opposite. His election is not grounded on his merits foreseen by God (compare Romans 9: 10–13). But Jacob is converted by the grace of God and becomes the father of the covenant people. Thus it will be through the children of Jacob that the Kingdom of God will be demonstrated.

The rest of the patriarchal story[4] takes us with Joseph and his brothers to Egypt, where the stage will be set for the next chapter in the history of redemption. The very fact that the descendants of Abraham are forced to go to Egypt for their welfare is also to be seen in the light of the covenant promises. For even when it appears (much to the dismay of the King of Egypt) that they are becoming a mighty nation, the land of promise is far off and inaccessible.

MOSES AND THE EXODUS – THE PROMISES ACTIVATED

The Exodus

'Now there arose a new king over Egypt, who did not know Joseph' (Exodus 1: 8). Suddenly the once favoured sons of Israel (Jacob) are no longer welcome guests in the fertile Nile delta. Sojourn becomes captivity and privilege becomes enslavement. The covenant promises are removed one stage further, for the people not only live away from the promised land, but are now prisoners of a cruel monarch. Again the experience of the recipients of the promises seems to contradict the promises. But from a more positive angle we can begin to put together some pieces of the puzzle. Why has God not fulfilled the promises? It is one thing to talk of faith, but faith is not to be confused with delusion and wishful thinking. The promises must be based on a reality which will be achieved if they are not to be a cruel hoax.

---

[4] The patriarchs are the 'fathers', i.e. Abraham, Isaac, Jacob and his twelve sons.

At this stage we can only observe that God must have a reason for creating this tension. To what purposes are the promises channelled through this extraordinary Egyptian experience? The Book of Exodus will show us the answer to this question. Exodus begins with the story of Moses' birth, preservation and preparation for his mission. These events are not only favourite subjects in Bible teaching programmes for children but are also frequently mishandled. The story of Moses in the rushes must be related to the declared purpose of God in Exodus 2: 23–25, which shows us that Moses is to be the mediator of God's acts in fulfilling the covenant promises made to the patriarchs. Notice the stress given to the identification of the God who sends Moses to be Israel's leader. He is the God of Abraham, Isaac and Jacob (Exodus 2: 24, 3: 6, 13, 15 and 16, 4: 5, 6:2–5).

That the God of Israel is the God who is faithful to the covenant with Abraham is a fact now associated with the personal name of God.[5] In most English versions of the Bible this holy name is translated LORD. Wherever you read LORD in your English Old Testament as the name of God remember it is his special personal name, and not merely a title – it expresses the character of God which has been revealed in his acts to redeem his people. The act and the knowledge of the name are frequently related: I will take you for my people . . . and you shall know that I am Jehovah (the LORD) your God (Exodus 6: 7, compare 7: 5).

So Israel is in bondage, through no obvious fault of her own, in Egypt far from Canaan. Now God acts on the basis of the covenant to release the children of Jacob. But Pharaoh is a cruel tyrant and refuses to let the people go. God, through his servant Moses, works a series of signs and wonders to make Pharoah release Israel. Each plague inflicted is a demonstration of the superior might of Jehovah over Egypt and its gods. The final plague is associated with a redemptive picture that Israel was never to forget. As God pronounces death upon all the first-born in Egypt, a way of escape is provided for believing Israelites. The sacrifice of a lamb and the sprinkling of its blood on the doorposts would cause the angel of death to pass over each household that complied. The Passover redemption of the Israelite firstborn is coupled with the escape from

[5] Exodus 6: 2–5 stresses the relationship of the name of God to his character as the covenant keeper. LORD is usually used to translate the Hebrew proper name YHVH from which the name Jehovah is derived. The Israelites at some stage ceased to pronounce this name because it was so holy

Egypt, so that the redemptive picture is extended to include all Israel. The effect of this tenth plague on Pharaoh is to cause him finally to let the people go. Up to this point his heart is hardened and even now he is to have second thoughts and pursue the fugitives to the Red Sea.[6]

The way out of Egypt would naturally be by the well-trodden way from the Delta through the coastal strip to Canaan But God does not lead them that way (Exodus 13: 17) but through the wilderness to the shores of the sea. This is like running into a blind-alley with walls on all sides. But God's purpose is still to be seen; he has already overcome the barrier of Pharaoh's hard heart and now he will overcome the barrier of the sea. It will not be by following the easy trade-route, but by the strong hand of God that Israel will come out of Egypt – redemption is a miracle that only God can perform (Exodus 6: 6b, 13: 9–16) Even the magicians of Egypt have recognized the finger of God at work (Exodus 8: 19).

Now we can answer the question we posed above: why has God not fulfilled the promises? Israel was brought to Egypt and the patriarchs never possessed the land, because God intended to reveal the way into his Kingdom. It is a way involving a miraculous redemption from a bondage that holds us and keeps us out of the Kingdom. Only a miracle of God can bring us back to the Kingdom. The Exodus will remain now the key model for the understanding of redemption in the life of Israel, and the people of God will be made to recall it as the basis of their response to a God who saves (see Exodus 20: 2, Deuteronomy 6: 20–25, 26: 5–10, Joshua 24: 6–13, Nehemiah 9: 6–12, Psalms 78, 105, 106, 114, 135 and 136).

The Sinai Covenant

The escaped Israelites came to Sinai where the next great aspect of Moses' ministry was to take place – the giving of the law. So much confusion has arisen at this point that we must endeavour to understand clearly the purpose of the law. Part of this confusion occurs because of a misunderstanding of the attitude to the law in the New Testament. Because Paul says of Christians, 'You are not

---

and instead substituted the word *ADONAI* (=my Lord). Hence the translation LORD.

[6] The Hebrew *Yam Suph* means Reed Sea not Red Sea. There is some dispute as to where Israel actually crossed the water, but this hardly affects the miraculous significance of the crossing.

under law but under grace' (Romans 6: 14), and because he stresses that justification means a righteousness which is 'apart from law' (Romans 3: 21), it is too easily assumed that the law is not only bypassed in the gospel, but even overthrown. It is not unfair, I think, to say that many Christians have an understanding something like this: God gave Israel the law at Sinai as a programme of works whose goal is salvation. The history of Israel shows how complete was the inability of Israel to achieve the required standard. God, therefore, in a kind of desperation, scrapped plan A (salvation through works of the law) and instituted as an emergency plan B (the gospel). The Old Testament thus becomes essentially the record of the failure of plan A. Its relationship to the New Testament is almost wholly negative.

In order to gain the right perspective on the Sinai law we must be more careful to examine the treatment of it in both Old Testament and New Testament. We must look at the positive statements about the law in the New Testament and also understand the reason for the many negative statements. If the depreciation of law in the New Testament is seen to apply not to law in itself, but to the perverted use of the law in Israel, the proper understanding and use of law will also be seen in the Old Testament.

To begin with, we acknowledge that two major events stand behind Sinai. The one is the Exodus and the other is the covenant with Abraham. If the Exodus means anything it means freedom from bondage. It is therefore clear that the law could not originate at Sinai as another form of bondage. The continuity of the declared purpose of God requires us to place Sinai in the context of the purposes of God to make a people for himself on the basis of his grace. The call and covenanting of Abraham was an act of grace. The descendants of Abraham were promised the kingdom by grace. The mighty acts of God in Egypt were performed because of the promise to Abraham (Exodus 2: 23–25). The Exodus event becomes a model of salvation by grace, its goal being the fulfilment of the promises to Abraham in the promised land. It is utterly inconceivable that God should break off his programme of salvation by grace in mid-stream (between Egypt and Canaan) and, despite his promises to Abraham, saddle his people with a frustrating programme of salvation by works! The narrative of Exodus does not allow such violence to be done to its theological continuity. The only reasonable assessment of the Sinai law in this context is that it is part of the programme of grace whereby God works to fulfil his promises to Abraham. This is no 'plan A' to be jettisoned later on, but part of a single, comprehensive plan God had from the beginning.

The heart of the law is the Ten Commandments (Exodus 20) which are prefaced by the significant phrase, 'I am the Lord your God, who brought you out of the land of Egypt, out of the house of bondage.' These words should govern our understanding of the Sinai law. Here we see that God declares that he is the God of this people, that he has already saved them. What follows then cannot be a programme aimed to achieve salvation by works since they have already received it by grace. The law is given to the people of God after they become the people of God by grace. Sinai is dependant upon the covenant with Abraham and is an exposition of it. At Sinai God spells out for his people what it means to be the people of God. They cannot know how to live consistently with their calling in life as Jehovah's people unless he tells them. What he does tell them reflects in various ways his own character. It is their faithful response to the character of God that will demonstrate that they are his children. The law explicates further the knowledge of God's character already revealed in his dealing with their fore-fathers and in his acts in Egypt (Exodus 6: 6–8).[7]

Given this understanding of the Sinai covenant, the moral prescriptions are easy enough to understand. But what of the ritual details and the many laws concerning what is clean and what unclean (especially with regard to food)? It is helpful to know something of the range of prescriptions given in Exodus and Leviticus, but the individual precepts should not be viewed apart from the context of the whole covenant. The sum total of the covenant of Sinai equals the great covenant summary: 'I will be your God and you will be my people.'[8] It explains in detail the

---

[7] This interpretation is supported by recent studies into treaty formulations in the Ancient Near East. It has been demonstrated with a fair degree of certainty that the form of the decalogue, i.e. the Ten Commandments, and possibly even the whole book of Deuteronomy, is the same as the conventional form of treaty covenants imposed by conquering kings on the conquered. These treaties set out the stipulations which governed the life of the vassal people as members of the great kingdom. If the analogy of 'form' holds, the use of this form for the decalogue would be appropriate only if the law of Sinai was intended to be a covenant which stipulated the conditions imposed upon the people made subjects of the God of the covenant.

[8] This particular summary statement occurs first in Leviticus 26: 12, but is also contained in the partial form given in Genesis 17: 7f, Exodus 6: 7. The significance of the declaration is highlighted by its repeated use through the

demands of the character of God: 'You shall be holy, for I the Lord your God am holy' (Leviticus 19: 2). The fact that many of its regulations do not touch directly the moral character of God stems from the nature of this preliminary revelation of God's kingdom. Some laws must deal with the national life of Israel, because that is where they are. Others are ritual requirements which depend on a later fulfilment for their full meaning. A group of apparently meaningless food laws become meaningful in the context of the Sinai covenant.[9] They instruct the people in one aspect of the unique relationship they possess as a holy people, separated from all other allegiance and separated to Jehovah.

The details for the building of the Tabernacle (Exodus 25–31) must be looked at in the light of the overall purpose of the Tabernacle and not be interpreted for their own sake. A secondary aspect of all the detail is that it expresses clearly the fact that Israel cannot be left to design things without God's revelation. What we might call the 'symbolic aids to worship' must conform to a given pattern, otherwise the heart of man will create something else which reflects not the character of God but only the evil inclinations of man's heart. For this very reason Israel is forbidden all forms of visual aids to worship and of pictures or images of God. Man is incapable of portraying God without falling into idolatry. The purpose of the Tabernacle is expressed as the dwelling of God (Exodus 29: 45) which means the symbol of God's presence among his people But on the other hand the barriers against access to the 'holy of holies' mean that a sinful people have only indirect access through the mediation of priests, and that only on the basis of substitutionary sacrifice for their sins.

Breaking the law carries heavy penalties, the most severe being death or excommunication. Israel as a nation is expected to be faithful to the law if it is also to enjoy the blessings of God. It is this fact (e.g. see Deuteronomy 28) which may be misinterpreted to

Bible, e.g. Exodus 29: 45, Jeremiah 24: 7, 31: 33 and 32: 38, Ezekiel 11: 20, 34: 24 and 37: 23, Zechariah 8: 8, II Corinthians 6: 16, Revelation 21: 3. The relationship expressed is the same that is included in the idea of the Kingdom of God.

[9] I cannot accept the view that the rationale behind food laws – what is clean for eating, and what is unclean and therefore forbidden – lies only in considerations of hygiene. Even if some aspects of hygiene may be detected these cannot be the main purpose. The 'passing away' of the food laws (e.g. Colossians 2: 16f) results from the coming of Christ, not from the invention of the refrigerator!

imply that the blessings of salvation are the reward for the works of the law. We should note however that the New Testament carries exactly the same conditions. And no New Testament teaching destroys the principle of salvation by grace (e.g. I Corinthians 6: 9–10 and 10: 6–12, Ephesians 4: 1, Hebrews 12: 12–17, James 1: 26–27, I John 3: 14–15). In both the Old and New Testaments the principle operates that the people of God should exhibit a holiness which is consistent with their calling. The deliberate flouting of this principle is clear demonstration that we are not members of God's people.[10] In both Testaments the demand to be holy stems from the prior saving activity of God. Much more could be said about the Sinai covenant but we must be content here with these few comments about its signifi cance and purpose.

THE ENTRY AND SETTLEMENT

The book of Numbers relates the incidents between Sinai and the entry. In so doing it presents a rather gloomy picture. Israel, which rides the crest of the wave of its salvation-experience in coming out of Egypt and in being constituted the people of God under the covenant of Sinai, is shown to be rebellious and ungrateful. The grumbling of the escaped nation becomes an immediate pattern (e.g Exodus 16–18). After the Sinai encounter the nation asserts its independence of God by refusing the opportunity to take possession of the promised land (Numbers 13–14). The forty years wandering in the wilderness disposes of the generation of adults who came out of Egypt, leaving their children to go in and possess the land.

Prior to the entry Moses relates the covenant to this anticipated possession of the land and then hands over his leadership to Joshua. This 'second law', as the name of the book of Deuteronomy signifies, once more emphasizes the gracious provision of God for his people as he fulfils the promises made to Abraham. This grace contrasts sharply with the rebelliousness of Israel in the wilderness.

---

[10] It is clear that in both Old and New Testaments we see a distinction between the root cause or basis of something, and the instrumental cause. Thus, we cannot be saved without faith, but on the other hand we are not saved because of faith. Faith is the instrument, but the basis of salvation is the righteousness of Christ. Likewise we cannot be saved without the new birth, yet the new birth is not the root cause or basis of salvation; if it were, Christ need never have died. The New Testament, as does the Old Testament, indicates that we cannot be saved *on the basis* of good works.

We may well wonder why God continues to show loving kindness to Israel despite the lack of response. Of course this is really no different from the question of why God shows grace to humanity at the Fall or to us today! Israel's rebelliousness is a recurring theme of the Old Testament, but so also is God's covenant love as he saves a remnant of faithful people out of the mass of the people. Indeed the remnant is an important theme which goes back to the beginning of redemptive history.[11] In the midst of all this rebellion the fact must not be overlooked that God is always saving the faithful remnant.

Deuteronomy is an important book as it emphasizes the relationship of law and grace. The first four chapters tell the story of salvation history, from the time spent at Sinai to the point of preparation to enter Canaan. The salvation history is interpreted in the light of Israel's faithlessness and of God's continuing kindness. Nowhere are law and gospel more clearly related than they are in Deuteronomy 6:20–25. The child asks, 'What does the law mean, what is it all about?', and the answer is given in terms of 'gospel', that is, in terms of what God did in history to save his people.[12] Does God act like this because Israel deserves it? Deuteronomy answers with a resounding 'No'. God 'loves because he loves' is the logic of Deuteronomy 7: 7–8. Israel is allowed to dispossess Canaan, not because Israel is worthy and merits it but because Canaan deserves judgement (Deuteronomy 9: 4–6). Always behind this is the promise of God to Abraham, to which God remains faithful despite Israel's rebelliousness (Deuteronomy 7: 8 and 9: 5).

[11] The separation of the godly line from the godless in Genesis 4–11 is the beginning of this process. As the pattern develops, we see that the remnant itself becomes the subject of a separation of a new remnant and so on. Thus from fallen humanity comes the godly line. From this comes the family of Noah, from Noah the family of Shem, from Shem the family of Abraham. Then comes the family of Isaac and Jacob. It is in this family of Israel that we now see the differentiation between the faithful response to the covenant and that of rebelliousness. In other words the membership of the covenant people on the basis of *birth* never guarantees automatically the *blessings* of the covenant.

[12] It cannot be stressed too much that the biblical expression of the gospel is an historical event as God acts on behalf of his people to save. The gospel is the holy history worked out in the life and death of Christ. The gospel is *not* man's response to this event, nor is it the work of God in us now as he regenerates and sanctifies the believer. So in the Old Testament the 'gospel' is the declaration of what God did 'out there' and 'back there' at a fixed place and time in history.

The book of Joshua takes up the history narrative from Deuteronomy as Joshua, the successor to Moses, prepares to lead Israel into the land. One cannot escape the emphasis here that God is about to act for Israel. The great acts of God for Israel in the Exodus are to be continued since salvation is not complete until the people are brought into the inheritance. Once again a miracle will allow the people to pass through the waters on dry ground (Joshua 3: 7–13). They will not need to sneak over in some remote area, but will cross opposite the great fortress city of Jericho (Joshua 3: 16). God will fight for them, not only in the destruction of Jericho and Ai, but in the subjugation of the whole land. And these events, which later pass into Israel's history, became part of the 'gospel of the mighty acts of God' along with the crossing of the Red Sea (Joshua 4: 21–23).

Thus the book of Joshua describes the process of dispossession of the various groups of Canaanites from their land by Israel. Although some pockets of resistance remain and troubles beset the Israelites from within the land and without, yet the assessment of the author may be accepted: 'The Lord gave Israel all the land which he had sworn to give to their forefathers; and having taken possession of it, they settled there. And the Lord gave them rest on every side just as he had sworn to their forefathers; not one of all their enemies had withstood them, for the Lord had given all their enemies into their hands. Not one of all the good promises which the Lord had made to the house of Israel had failed; all came to pass' (Joshua 21: 43–45). Again we note that this fulfilment of the gracious promises in the saving acts of God is not to be divorced from the covenant's demands upon Israel. Joshua calls upon the people to remember the serious consequences of transgressing the covenant (Joshua 23: 14–16). The book ends with a moving account of a covenant renewal ceremony which again stresses the gospel of what God has done for his people (Joshua 24: 2–13), and which describes the demand upon the people to respond with faithful obedience (verses 14–27).

THE PROGRESS TOWARDS MONARCHY – JUDGESHIP

We must be brief in describing this most detailed area of Israel's historical narrative. The period covers more than two centuries of the most important developments in the national life of Israel. The book of Judges records a certain instability which may on first sight appear to contradict the glowing terms used in Joshua 21: 43–45. However, Judges does not deny that God gave all the land into Israel's hand, but rather stresses the fact that the tribes of Israel were slack in following through the instructions to utterly drive the inhabitants out. By tolerating little pockets of the enemy within the land, they weakened their position and the way was opened for difficult times ahead.

The theology of the book of Judges is summarized in Chapter 2. Contact with the enemy was always dangerous, not only because it could threaten national security, but principally because it threatened the integrity of Israel's faith. Both situations threatened the covenant. Again it is clear that the whole process of covenant fulfilment is being worked out at the level of national existence in a way which does not succeed in bringing the whole realm of human existence into the Kingdom. To put it another way, Israel's experiences show the way God acts and what the Kingdom is like, but as people the Israelites remain sinful and rebellious. We do not see the whole nation submitting perfectly and willingly to God's rule. This fact will shape our understanding of the extent to which the Kingdom of Israel exhibits the truth of the Kingdom of God.

So in Judges 2: 11–23 we find the theological interpretation of the events of the whole book. The stories of the heroic deeds of Ehud, Gideon, Samson and the other judges, are stories of 'mini-salvations'. The same cycle is there in each case – Israel's sin, judgement at the hand of the enemy, Israel's repentance and call for help, and the saviour judge who rescues Israel from the enemy. Every victory under the leadership of one of these judges is a saving act of God by which he establishes the people in their inheritance. From our perspective these repetitions of salvation may seem to disrupt the harmony of the overall historical events in revealing salvation and the Kingdom. But we must recognize that God's loving kindness is at work in the generations following the Exodus from Egypt, repeatedly showing his saving mercy. This period does not become too complicated as long as we maintain a perspective on the major events and their theological significance in revealing the kingdom. The account of this period of upheaval comes to an end with the significant statement: 'In those days there was no king in Israel; every man did what was right in his own eyes' (Judges 21: 25). If this indicates that the author is looking back on these events from the time of the monarchy, it also indicates that he sees the monarchy as necessary to provide stability and order in Israel.

SAMUEL AND SAUL

From the fragmentation of national life and the localized activity of
the judges there develops a movement towards a more coherent and
structured situation. Samuel the prophet-judge figures prominently
in this trend. He is accepted as a prophet, the first national
prophetic figure since Moses, from Dan to Beersheba (I Samuel 3:
19–20).[13] The enemy now is the Philistine nation. The leadership of
Samuel during this extreme threat puts him in the path of a new
political development. The Israelites perceive the advantage of
stable government and, following the example of the neighbouring
states, demand a king to rule over them and to lead them in battle
(I Samuel 8: 19–20).

That the motives of the Israelites in asking for a king are all
wrong can be seen in the nature of their expectations which are
political and military rather than truly religious (verse 20). The
request is seen as a rejection of God's rule (I Samuel 8: 7). However,
this does not indicate that kingship was not in God's purpose, nor
does it mean that kingship is granted solely as a rope for the people
to hang themselves. We must distinguish between the kind of
kingship asked for and the kind of kingship which lay in God's
purposes. If the people hang themselves, it is by means of Saul. Saul
is God's answer to the wrong motives of the Israelites, but at the
same time the opportunity remains for Saul to prove himself and to
succeed as God's anointed.

Kingship as such was already a permitted possibility in the words
of Moses. In Deuteronomy 17: 14–20 we have the pattern of true
kingship which is fully consistent with the theocratic ideals of Sinai.
Essentially this king exemplifies the law in his life and does not lift
up his heart above his brethren (verse 20). He is contrasted with the
oriental despotic monarch who uses his position for personal
aggrandizement and exercises an absolute power which is inconsis-
tent with theocracy (verses 16–17). It would appear that Samuel has
this Deuteronomic prescription for kingship in mind when he
warns the people of the folly of desiring to be ruled by a despo
(I Samuel 8: 10–18). He understands only too well that political
stability can be bought at a very heavy price; the 'law and order'
ticket has been the crowd-winner for dictators all through the ages.

---

[13] These two towns represent the extreme north and the extreme south of
the land respectively, and thus express the truly national, rather than local,
nature of Samuel's influence.

The pattern of Saul's behaviour may be discerned very early in his reign. He appears with all the charisma of the hero warriors that we know as judges (I Samuel 10: 23–24, 11: 5–15), but also with all the seeds of corruption and of rejection of his theocratic position as the Lord's anointed (I Samuel 13: 13–14, 15: 10–31). Samuel, as prophet, remains the Lord's spokesman and brings the word of judgement against the disobedient Saul. This relationship of prophet to king will persist throughout the monarchy in Israel, for the prophet is ever the guardian of the covenant of Sinai against which the lives of all Israelites are measured.

Positively, then, Saul is one mere link in a chain of historical figures who represent the purpose of God to administer salvation through a human mediator. Saul's significance as the 'Lord's anointed' becomes of prime importance to David so that, even when Saul is seeking to kill David, he will not retaliate. However imperfectly he does it, Saul brings a coherence to rulership in Israel that has not existed since the wilderness days. We should not let the negative elements in Saul detract from the positive significance of his reign. It is characteristic of the Old Testament persons and events that despite their imperfections, they foreshadow the perfect which is to come (I Cor. 13: 10). In fact it must be this, for if the foreshadowings were perfect they would no longer be mere shadows and would become the solid reality. Saul, along with the judges before him, and the kings after him, is part of the historical foundation laid in the Old Testament for the revelation of the perfect human king, Jesus of Nazareth, who mediates God's rule.

DAVID

The length of Saul's reign is difficult to ascertain and the narrative does not dwell on it longer than to indicate the salient features. However, Saul's rejection by the prophet Samuel (Samuel 13: 14, 15: 26–28) serves not so much as the precursor of Saul's death as of the introduction of Saul's successor David. 'The Lord repented that he had made Saul king over Israel' (I Samuel 15: 35) is the preface to the events in chapter 16.

For the second time Samuel is called upon to designate the Lord's anointed. This time the narrative describes with great dramatic effect the choice of Jesse's youngest son as the man after God's own heart (I Samuel 13: 14). Since this takes place long before Saul's death, the story records the drawn-out rivalry between the two men that ends only with Saul's suicide in the battle of Gilboa. During this period from the anointing of David to the death of Saul the narrative focuses not on Saul but upon David as the up-and-coming ruler.

The first major event recorded in David's experience as the anointed one, is his slaying of Goliath (I Samuel 17). Here we see another part of the transition from judge-saviour to king-saviour. David, the anointed one, challenges the enemy of God's people and kills the giant with the same result as the victories of the judges. It is a saving event in which the chosen mediator wins the victory, while the ordinary people stand by until they can share in the fruits of the saviour's victory. Preparation is thus made for the gospel events in which God's Christ (Anointed One) wins the victory over sin and death on behalf of his people.

Until the death of Saul increasing tension between himself and David shows Saul's appalling jealousy of the one chosen to succeed him. David, by contrast, is completely subdued by his regard for Saul's office as the anointed king. Though persecuted by Saul and forced to roam the wilderness with a band of outlaws, David steadfastly refuses to pre-empt the sovereignty of God by killing the Lord's anointed (I Samuel 24: 4–6, 26: 8–11). The hapless Amalekite, who seeks to curry favour with David by claiming to have killed his persecutor, learns the hard way the strength of David's convictions in this matter (2 Samuel 1: 14–16). Again we can distinguish part of the pattern-making aspect of those events in the rejection and suffering of the king-designate before he is vindicated and raised to the throne to rule in glory.

David's reign continues to exhibit the mixture of theocratic ideal and human sinfulness that has characterized salvation history. Indeed if it were not for the prophetic assessments of David made after his death, in which the ideals of God's rule through human kingship are stressed, we might wonder at times if David is much of an improvement upon Saul. Certainly his rule sees a growth in prosperity and the stabilizing of the whole political, economic and military scene. But even that aspect, as we well know from the ministry of Samuel, is full of potential for evil. Furthermore, the portrayal of David as an adulterer and murderer hardly enhances the theocratic ideal!

In order to maintain the proper perspective on David we must preserve the framework of the covenant and salvation history. The stability and prosperity achieved by David in finally removing the threat of Philistine incursion into the promised land, and also in rooting out the last pockets of Canaanite influence, represent fulfilment of the covenant promises. Now some substance is given to the covenant summary, 'I will be your God, you shall be my people'.

It is at this point that a new prophetic word is heard, giving an important perspective on the significance of David. Now that the wanderings of Israel have ceased and the people possess the land as promised to Abraham, the obvious symbol of God's dwelling would be a permanent temple rather than the portable tent-tabernacle. Such a temple is eventually built by Solomon, but at this juncture an important clue is given to the way in which the tabernacle-temple symbolism will reach its true fulfilment in God's kingdom. Nathan's prophecy to David (II Samuel 7) is in a sense a word out of due time, for it anticipates a prophetic perspective which does not fully emerge until the latter prophets, beginning with Amos and Hosea.

The following key points emerge from Nathan's prophecy in II Samuel 7:

(a) David proposes to build God a dwelling, yet this has never been commanded by God (verses 5–7).
(b) God declares that he will build a house for David as he gives rest to his people (verses 8–11).
(c) This house is a dynasty of David's royal descendants and David's son will build God's dwelling (verses 12–13).[14]
(d) David's son will be the personal embodiment of the people of God and is declared to be God's son (verse 14).[15]

There is much more that could be said about David's reign, but we must be content with these few theological aspects and turn to the significance of Solomon as David's son.

SOLOMON

The first and obvious point to note about Solomon is that as the son of David he fulfils in an immediate sense Nathan's prediction that

[14] There is a play here on the Hebrew word *bayit*. On the one hand it signifies *house* meaning 'dwelling', and on the other it signifies *house* meaning 'household' or 'dynasty'.
[15] It is reasonable to suggest that 'I will be his father, and he shall be my son' is an individualizing of the covenant statement 'I will be your God and

the house of God would be built by such a son. But Solomon must be remembered for more than his temple building activity. In fact he is an enigma, for he was both the perfecter of Israel's glory and the architect of its destruction.

The form of the narrative of Solomon's reign in I Kings is instructive. The problem of the throne succession having been settled in Solomon's favour, the narrator deals at once with two apparently contradictory aspects of Solomon's behaviour. First we are told of the marriage alliance with the king of Egypt (I Kings 3: 1), which becomes a cause of stumbling in that it is the first stage of the apostasy described in Chapter 11: 1–13. Secondly we are told of Solomon's desire for an understanding mind – a request which receives God's commendation.

The wisdom of Solomon and the splendour of his kingdom go hand in hand, and both are seen as undergirding national prosperity and safety: 'Judah and Israel dwelt in safety, from Dan to Beersheba, every man under his vine and under his fig tree, all the days of Solomon' (I Kings 4: 25). So the writer sums up the situation in a way that suggests that the prosperity of Solomon's reign is indicative of the fulfilment of the promises to Abraham. The people are in the land, they are safe, and the land yields its fruit in Eden-like plenty.

Solomon's wisdom, at first sight, is found in strange company. 'God gave Solomon wisdom and understanding beyond measure, and largeness of mind like the sand of the seashore, so that Solomon's wisdom surpassed the wisdom of all the people of the east, and all the wisdom of Egypt' (I Kings 4: 29–30). Clearly Solomon's wisdom was of a kind that might be compared with that of pagans. The narrative describes the 'wise men' of other lands coming to hear Solomon (chapter 4: 34), as well as the adulation of the Phoenician king Hiram (chapter 5: 7), and of the Queen of Sheba who came to test Solomon's wisdom (chapter 10: 1–5).

We know from the book of Proverbs that 'wisdom' was seen as concerned with the complexities of daily life and with the real world of human experience. As such it would naturally be a concern of all men, Israelite and pagan alike. Perhaps it was this very worldliness of the wisdom of Solomon (see I Kings 4: 32–33) that made it possible for a wise man to move from a wisdom guarded by the framework of the 'fear of the Lord' (Proverbs 1: 7) into a wisdom

---

you shall be my people'. David's line is thus declared to be representative of God's people or, to put it another way, David's son is the true Israel.

which spoke of the same things but which forgot the revealed will of God.

So Solomon, who beautified Israel with the Temple (I Kings 7 and 8), becomes the apostate from whom the kingdom is removed with a word that recalls the rejection of Saul – 'I will surely tear the kingdom from you and give it to your servant' (I Kings 11: 11). The story which follows is a long one which leads firstly to the division of the kingdom with the revolt of the northern tribes against Rehoboam, and then to the decline and fall of both North and South.

We must be content here to point out only the salient feature of the history of the divided kingdom. Both the kingdom of Israel and the kingdom of Judah move with gathering momentum towards a cataclysmic judgement of God upon their sinful rejection of the covenant. The final outcome of Solomon's apostasy is the obliteration of the natural existence of Israel. All that the covenant to Abraham had promised was under Solomon both realized and lost. To say this is to say that the realization of the promises must be qualified by all the deficiencies due to human sinfulness. In whatever sense the Kingdom of God is fulfilled in Solomon's reign, something is yet lacking. The pattern of Kingdom existence is certainly there, but its perfection is not. If the united Kingdom fulfils the covenant promises it does so only in shadow. So if God is faithful, the solid substance of that fulfilment must be yet to come. Such is the message of the prophets.

CHAPTER EIGHT

The Kingdom Revealed in Prophecy

THE 'OLD ORDER' PROPHETS

FOR THE PURPOSES OF OUR DISCUSSION WE MAY DIVIDE THE PROPHETS of Israel into two main groups. The first group comprises the prophets who live in the period of the Kingdom in history (as described in Chapter 7) and whose message is mainly orientated to that epoch of revelation. The second group consists of those living in the period after the schism between Judah and Israel when the history of Israel ceases to contribute positively to the revelation of the Kingdom.

We may note that the first group contains the 'non-writing' prophets while the second group contains the 'writing' prophets.[1] It is reasonable to ask why the later prophets, from Amos on, have their oracles preserved in books while the earlier ones are known only in the context of wider historical narratives. The answer may well lie partly in the fact that the writing prophets belong to a new epoch of revelation of the Kingdom of God and consequently there is a greater need for the new revelation to be preserved in a formal way.

The 'old order' prophets belong to the Kingdom of God as it is revealed in Israel's history. The definitive prophet of this period is Moses (see Deuteronomy 18: 15–22, 34: 10–12 and Numbers 12:

---

[1] This terminology is not precise since it is not at all clear how much of the prophetic literature was actually written by the prophets themselves. Essentially the prophetic oracle was a spoken word and its committal to writing was a subsequent event.

6–8). In the Old Testament a variety of activities are described as prophetic so that we must avoid being simplistic in the description of the prophetic office. Nevertheless it is fair to say that a prophet was essentially one who was called to communicate God's revelation to men. This is the aspect that we now consider.

In the epoch of Kingdom revelation in Israel's history, it is Moses who mediates (i.e. communicates) the declared purpose of God to save Israel out of Egypt, and who is God's instrument in carrying out this purpose. Later, it is Moses who receives the covenant law of Sinai by which the people are constituted as the people of God's kingdom. The entire history of the fulfilment of God's promises to Abraham, as it is worked out from Moses to Solomon, is regulated by the Kingdom ideal contained in the Sinai covenant. The history of Israel in the promised land is given its meaning within the framework of the promise to Abraham, the release from Egypt, and the covenant of Sinai.

All the prophets after Moses stand as the watchdogs of the society of God's people, working always within the framework of the covenant of Sinai. The prophets hold the law as a mirror so that individuals and the whole nation may see how they transgress. They call people back to faithful obedience to the covenant and, when necessary, denounce the unbelief and disobedience of their day.

The prophetic office is closely related to the conditions laid down for enjoyment of the covenant blessings. Although Israel's salvation has for its basis God's gracious acts in saving the people out of Egypt, there is a close link between enjoyment of the final outcome of salvation and Israel's obedience. At first sight this appears to mean that Israel's salvation is achieved by obedience to the law, but this is not so. Grace comes first in the saving acts of God, then law binds the saved people to God as his people. Should these people refuse to accept their responsibility to live as God's people, then they must suffer removal from the land of blessing.[2] This

---

[2] The relationship of good works to salvation is essentially the same in both Old and New Testaments. In both salvation is by grace, but grace never stands alone without good works. To put it another way we may say that no-one (in Old or New Testaments) is saved *because* of good works, but no-one is saved *without* good works. This is one aspect of the unity of the two Testaments which makes the Old Testament so applicable to Christians. The same unity underlies Paul's use of the exodus situation in I Corinthians 10: 1–12.

conditional nature of blessing is clearly set out in many parts of the Sinai covenant, not least in the Ten Commandments (Exodus 20: 5–6, 7 and 12) and in Deuteronomy (for example see Deuteronomy 11: 26–32, 28: 1–68, 30: 15–20).

Samuel, Nathan, Gad, Ahijah and Shemaiah are among the prophets of the age of prophecy stretching from Moses to Elijah and Elisha. All of these men are orientated towards the Sinai covenant and the maintenance of the Kingdom of God as it is meant to be expressed in the history of Israel. Even when the kingdom of Israel is divided and begins on the slippery down-grade to destruction, the overlapping ministries of Elijah and Elisha combine in an effort to bring the people of God back to the covenant obedience. In keeping with this here-and-now concern of the prophets we find that their words of judgement and grace are worked out in the context of the present Kingdom epoch.

PRE-EXILIC PROPHETS

With the ministry of Amos we enter into a new period of prophecy which both continues certain features of the old order and also introduces some significant new characteristics. While we must be careful not to oversimplify the prophetic message, it is possible to discern a distinct development in emphasis particularly in the prophetic view of eschatology[3] or the end time.

Transgression of the Law

There are three essential ingredients in the oracles of these latter prophets. First there is the covenant of Sinai which remains the rule of faith and behaviour. This God-given law is never considered a temporary thing. It stands as the expression of God's character which is unchanging, and as such it is the point of reference when the prophets interpret events as God's dealings with Israel. Against this law the conduct of the covenant people is seen to be lacking and a terrible provocation towards God. Whatever specific aspect of transgression the individual prophets concentrate

---

[3] The study of the last things (*eschatos* means 'last' in Greek) or of the end of the age.

on, the underlying implications are always the same – Israel (or Judah) has broken covenant with the merciful God who saved this people for himself.

Amos, for example, emphasizes social injustices: Amos 1: 6–8, 4: 1–3, 5: 10–13, 8: 4–6. Isaiah's opening chapters detail the formalism of Israel's worship as well as outright idolatry and apostasy. Ezekiel stresses the apostasy in Judah before the final destruction of Jerusalem in 586 B.C. The prophets do not really differentiate between social and religious sins any more than the Sinai covenant does. All sin is transgression of the covenant.

Judgement

Secondly, the prophets are the dutiful mediators of the message of judgement. The particularizing of covenant-breaking in the accusations against various forms of evil-doing is the grounds for the pronouncement of impending judgement. Insofar as these prophets are still orientated to the present Kingdom epoch, there is a conditional element to the message which indicates that repentance and faithful obedience may yet avert the judgement. More and more, however, the prophets present a picture of a terrible and final judgement. This aspect partly reflects the reality of the situation in that history gave no grounds for optimism. Given the pattern of rebelliousness that can be discerned from the very moment Israel is saved from the Egyptian captivity (Exodus 15: 22–24, 16: 1–3. See also Psalm 95: 8–11), there is little basis for confidence in the outcome unless this sinful bent of human character is taken care of. Consequently we notice a growing sense of the inevitable course of history towards the self-destruction of the covenant people. Even the most concerted efforts at reform are powerless to correct the situation (see II Kings 23: 24–27).

The form of the judgement to come is described in various ways but we may discern two emphases. One is to depict *a fairly immediate and local judgement* of God, and even retrospectively to point to *past events* as warning judgments (Amos 4: 6–11). In the northern kingdom of Israel the approaching doom is pin-pointed as the Assyrian invasion which subsequently brought about the end of that nation in 722 B.C. (Hosea 9: 1–6, 10: 5–10, 11: 5). In Judah the fate of Israel is cited as a warning and example (Isaiah 10: 10–11, Ezekiel 16: 51, 23: 1–11) and a similar fate at the hands of Babylon is predicted (Isaiah 39, Jeremiah 1: 13–16, 20: 4–6, 22: 24–27). The other emphasis is to portray judgement as something which is *of universal or cosmic proportions* (Jeremiah 4: 23–26, Isaiah 2: 2–22, 13: 5–10, 24: 1–23, Nahum 1: 4–6, Habakkuk 3: 3–12, Zephaniah 1: 2–3, 18, 3: 8, Ezekiel 38: 19–23).

We cannot separate these emphases of the judgement oracles as if the prophets clearly distinguished the judgement upon Israel and Judah from universal judgement. From our vantage point in time we see separate historical events – the destruction of Samaria in 722 B.C. and the destruction of Jerusalem in 586 B.C. – and we may anticipate a future final judgement. But we must not think that the failure of prophecy to distinguish clearly between these two aspects is due purely to a lack of historical perspective. Theologically all these manifestations of judgement are inextricably bound together. God's judgement of sin in the covenant people is not in principle different from his judging sin in all humanity.

Salvation

The third major element in prophetic preaching is the declaration that God is faithful to the covenant and on that basis he will save a remnant of the people to be his own true possession. Like the judgement oracles, the salvation oracles depict two related aspects of saving restoration. God will restore the covenant people to their inheritance and he will also restore the whole universe to a glory which has not been known since man was ejected from Eden. We will reserve a detailed discussion of the salvation oracles until later in this chapter when we look at the kingdom pattern in prophecy.

The Nations

There is another prominent feature in prophetic preaching which demands comment. Although little evidence exists outside the Book of Jonah that prophets ever preached to the Gentiles, there are many recorded oracles directed against the nations although preached to Israel or Judah. In fact these oracles are of such significance that they have sometimes been collected and presented as a group in the formation of the prophetic books (So Amos 1–2, Isaiah 13–23, Jeremiah 46–51, Ezekiel, 25–32).

The judgement against the nations is part of the overall judgement of God against sin which is noted above. We should also note, however, the relationship of judgement to salvation. In

judging the nations God is putting down all rebellion against him.
This activity is integral to the establishing of the Kingdom of God.
Thus the judgement of the nations is seen not only as part of general
judgement but also as the accompaniment of the salvation of God's
people. God is the warrior who fights for his people and rescues
them from captivity and oppression (Exodus 14: 14, 15: 3–6,
Deuteronomy 9: 3–5, Psalm 68). He will judge the nations for
having directed their ungodliness at God's own people (Joel 3:
1–21, Habakkuk 3: 6–13, Zephaniah 2: 5–15, Haggai 2: 21–23,
Jeremiah 46: 27–28, 50: 29–34, 51: 24).

THE EXILIC AND POST-EXILIC PROPHETS

The exilic prophets, Ezekiel and Daniel[4], are those who ministered
to the exiles in Babylon. The post-exilic prophets, Haggai,
Zechariah and Malachi, ministered to the restored community after
the return from Babylon. We note them here only to point out that,
with the Babylonian catastrophe either a present reality or a past
event, these prophets place a greater emphasis on the universal and
final acts of God both in salvation and judgement. It is during this
period that a new way of expressing future expectations is
developed in the form of *apocalyptic*.

Actually most Jewish apocalyptic writings appeared in the period
between the two testaments, but some elements of it may be
discerned in Daniel and Zechariah.[5] In the visions of Daniel
chapter 7 and 8 and Zechariah chapters 1 to 6 many apocalyptic
characteristics are seen, including symbolism and bizarre imagery.
More important for this discussion is the highly developed sense
that the present age will end and a new age will be introduced in
which God's kingdom is established. The Kingdom is seen as God's
new creation which cannot be brought in by reformation, but only
by a radical upheaval of the whole created order.

Just as the pre-exilic prophets had to interpret the failure of
Solomon's kingdom and project the hope of the believer for the
Kingdom of God into the future, the post-exilic prophets were

---

[4] We include Daniel among the prophets although in the Hebrew Old
Testament this book is not placed with the other prophetic books. (See also
Chapter Three, note 1).
[5] For a discussion of the characteristics of apocalyptic see Leon Morris:
Apolcalyptic (London: IVP, 1972) or articles in any Bible dictionary.

given the task of interpreting the manifest failure of the return from exile to produce the Kingdom. Once again the human cause is identified as sin, and the remedy is to be a final and decisive intervention of God in the future.

THE KINGDOM PATTERN IN PROPHECY

Now we return to the pattern of future hope to which all the writing prophets contributed. It may be summed up quite simply – the form of future history will be a replay of past history but with a significant difference. All the hope for the future is expressed in terms of a return to the Kingdom structures revealed in the history of Israel from the Exodus to Solomon. The great difference is that none of the weaknesses of the past will be present. In short, sin and its effects will be eradicated.

The prophets depict a continuity from the past to the future as well as a distinction between them. All that God has revealed about his Kingdom through Israel's history remains valid. But it is modified to the extent that the new view of the Kingdom leaves no place for a further disruption and decline. The restored Kingdom will be in the context of a new heaven and a new earth, and all this new creation of God will be permanent, perfect and glorious.

The simplest way to demonstrate this characteristic of prophetic hope is to list the ingredients of Israel's history which add up to the pattern of the Kingdom of God and then show how these are repeated in the prophetic futurism. In the previous chapter we saw the following features:

  i. Captivity as a contradiction to the Kingdom.
  ii. The Exodus events as God's mighty act of salvation on the basis of the Abrahamic covenant.
  iii. The Sinai covenant binding Israel to God as his people.
  iv. The entry and possession of Canaan.
  v. The focusing of God's rule through the Temple, the Davidic king, and the city of Jerusalem.

Why does God move at all to do a work of salvation for a rebellious nation? From the point of view of the Old Testament it is because he is faithful to his covenant made with Abraham as an everlasting covenant (Genesis 17: 7). God wills to show steadfast love or covenant love to his chosen people (Isaiah 54: 7–8, 55: 3, Jeremiah 33: 10–11, Micah 7: 18–20).[6]

Now on the basis of this covenant love God is doing a new work, and each of the features of the historic kingdom revelation will be renewed in the last days when God acts finally for salvation.

1. The new captivity The predictions of the pre-exilic prophets that Judah will be devastated and the people taken to Babylon provide a very obvious analogy with the Egyptian captivity, which is not overlooked. There is one new development. The reason for this captivity is clearly stated as sin or transgression of the covenant.

2. The new exodus The pattern of the Egyptian exodus is recalled in many oracles of the return from Babylon (Jeremiah 16: 14–15, 23: 7–8, Isaiah 43: 15–21). A number of passages in Isaiah allude to the exodus from Egypt in describing the coming exodus from Babylon (Isaiah 40: 3–4, 41: 17–20, 42: 7, 43: 1–2, 16–20, 48: 20–21, 49: 24–26, 51: 9–11, 52: 3–4, 11–12, 61–1).

3. The new covenant From one point of view it is accurate to say that the prophets see a renewal of several covenants – the Noahic (Isaiah 54: 8–10), the Abrahamic (Isaiah 49: 5–9, Jeremiah 33: 25–26), the Mosaic (Jeremiah 31: 31–36) and the Davidic (Jeremiah 33: 19–26). But it is easy to see from Jeremiah 33: 19–26 that the Abrahamic and Davidic covenants are closely related. There is in fact an essential unity to all the covenants. Jeremiah shows the unity between the Mosaic covenant and the new covenant (chapter 31: 31–34), for the new covenant is not a new thing replacing the old, but rather the old renewed and applied in such a way that it will be perfectly kept.

4. The new nation The prophets predict the return of a renewed people, a faithful remnant. This is a people whose heart is changed and to whom a new spirit is given so that law is fulfilled within them (Isaiah 10: 20–22, 46: 3–4, 51: 11, Jeremiah 23: 3, 31: 7, Ezekiel 36: 25–28). Then God will establish the nation in the land and Zion will be rebuilt (Isaiah 44: 24–28, 46: 13, 49: 14–21, 51: 3, 60: 3–14). The new Temple in Zion will be glorious (Ezekiel 40–47) and it will be a work of the spirit of God (Zechariah 4: 6–9). In accordance with the

---

[6] The Hebrew word *hesed* is commonly translated *mercy* or *steadfast love*. It is a technical term which expresses the idea of faithfulness to a covenant bond. Consequently it is a favourite word evoking praise and thanksgiving from the faithful as they contemplate God's covenant faithfulness. See, for example, Psalm 136 where each verse contains the refrain 'for his *hesed* endures for ever'.

covenant with David (II Samuel 7), the new David will reign as God's shepherd king over his people (Isaiah 11: 1, Jeremiah 23: 5–8, 33: 14–26, Ezekiel 34: 11–13, 23–25, 37: 24–28). And when all this glory of the new Zion is revealed, the nations will also receive a blessing in accordance with the promise to Abraham (Gen. 12: 3, cf. Isa. 2: 2–4, Micah 4: 1–4, Zech. 8: 20–23).

5. *The new creation* We have already seen that there is a continuity between the Kingdom of God revealed in Eden and the Kingdom of God revealed in Israel's history. It is therefore not surprising that the prophets occasionally refer to the Edenic kingdom as the pattern for the new kingdom to come, and even mingle elements of Eden and Canaan. Isaiah speaks of the redemption of Israel in the framework of the new creation, new heaven and a new earth (Isaiah 65: 17–21). In the context of this cosmic re-creation the new Jerusalem is a new Eden in which the harmony of nature is restored (cf. Isaiah 11: 1–9). All the references to the deserts becoming fertile recall the expectations that Canaan would be a land flowing with milk and honey – an imagery borrowed from Eden (see Isaiah 41: 18–20). God will make Zion's wilderness like Eden (Isaiah 51: 3, Ezekiel 36: 33–36).

POSTSCRIPT

When Judah is restored after the Persian takeover in 538 B.C., the situation is to all intents and purposes set for the great day of salvation predicted by the prophets. In fact such fulfilment of prophecy as does take place is only a pale shadow of the expectation. The books of Ezra and Nehemiah, along with Haggai, Zechariah, and Malachi, give quite a clear picture of the reconstruction. All the ingredients of the Kingdom promises are there but, far from exceeding the former glory, they do not come anywhere near to even matching it. Hence the need for the post-exilic prophets to explain why this is not the hoped-for day, and to project hope into the future yet again. This hope is often to flicker like a candle in the wind as year after year sees change but never true release from the oppressive domination of foreigners.

After the close of the Old Testament era during the Persian ascendancy the Jews underwent many trials. More than once the covenant faith was seriously threatened by pagan philosophies and lifestyles. The Temple was desecrated by Hellenists and many martyrs shed their blood.[7] Jewish faith developed different expressions through numbers of sects – Pharisees, Sadducees, Zealots, Essenes – while power in the Near East changed hands from the Persians to the Greeks and finally to the might of Imperial Rome. Through it all a faithful remnant waited for the consolation of Israel.

[7] Alexander the Great brought Greek power and culture into the biblical world towards the end of the fourth century B.C. After his death in 323 there was continual strife and rivalry for power until the advent of the Romans. The conflict of Hellenism with the faith of the Jews is well illustrated in the apocryphal books of I and II Maccabees.

CHAPTER NINE

The Kingdom Revealed in Jesus Christ

MOST CHRISTIANS HAVE SOME IDEA OF A LINK BETWEEN THE OLD Testament and the New Testament. For many it amounts to little more than a belief that some messianic prophecies were fulfilled by the coming of Jesus. In Chapter 2 we saw that any recognition of a unity of the whole Bible demands that we seek to know what kind of unity exists in order to be able to relate the Old to the New. In Chapter 3 we saw that being a Christian implies a certain method of approach to the unity of the Bible. To be a Christian is to recognize in Jesus Christ the goal of all things including the goal of the history of redemption. Because Jesus Christ is the perfect image of God (Colossians 1: 15–20, 2: 9–10, Hebrews 1: 3) we see him as the one towards whom all the former revelation of God is leading, and in whom it is fulfilled and given its meaning.

That the Old Testament anticipates the New and is fulfilled in the New is underlined by many general statements of the New Testament:

> 'In many and various ways God spoke of old to our fathers by the prophets; but in these last days he has spoken to us by a Son, whom he appointed the heir of all things' (Hebrews 1: 1–12). 'For all the promises of God find their Yes in him' (II Corinthians 1: 20).
> 'We bring you the good news that what God promised to the fathers, this he has fulfilled to us their children by raising Jesus' (Acts 13: 32–33).

'Beginning with Moses and all the prophets, he interpreted to them in all the scriptures the things concerning himself' (Luke 24: 27).

It is important that we understand very clearly that this fact of the Old Testament's progression towards a fulfilment in the New is not merely an invitation to understand Jesus Christ as the end of the process. It is also a demand that the whole Bible be understood in the light of the gospel. It means that Jesus Christ is the key to the interpretation of the whole Bible, and the task before us is to discern *how* he interprets the Bible. It should be realized at the outset that when we speak of Jesus Christ as the key to interpretation we must speak of Jesus Christ as he is revealed – the Christ of the gospel. It is not sufficient to stress the ethics of the man Jesus of Nazareth out of the context of the saving acts of God (as many liberals do), nor to stress the supernatural presence of the Christ with the believer out of the context of the meaning of the historical humanity of God come in the flesh (as many evangelicals do). Obviously we need to be clear about the gospel itself if we are to be clear about the significance of Christ for interpreting the Bible.

THE GOSPEL

What is the gospel? Pick any ten Christians and ask them this question and you will probably get ten different answers. Perhaps none of them will be wholly wrong, but the difference will suggest a certain confusion. Take two extremes to illustrate. The liberal Christian often stresses the *humanity* of Jesus. Jesus was a good man, in fact the only truly good man. The gospel of the good man must be reduced to some kind of example to follow, a demonstration inviting us to try to do likewise. There is obviously some truth in this view. On the other hand the evangelical often stresses the *divinity* of Jesus. The Christ is the supernatural Son of God who is alive today in the hearts of believers. The gospel of the divine Christ tends to be one of the supernaturally changed life. And there is obviously some truth in that.

Let us be clear on this point. To suggest that these two views are extremes containing some of the truth is not in any way at all to propose that we need a balance or a middle road which recognizes a little of each extreme. It is rather an invitation to come to grips with the biblical perspective.

Essentially the gospel is a declaration of what God has done *for* us in Jesus Christ, rather than (as is often implied) what God does in the believer, although we may not separate the two. It is the objective historical facts of the coming of Jesus in the flesh and the God-given interpretation of those facts. When Peter preached the gospel at Pentecost he was quick to divert attention from what God had done in the apostles by the giving of the Holy Spirit, and to concentrate on the facts concerning Jesus of Nazareth (Acts 2: 14–36).

The facts are those of the incarnation, of the perfect life of Jesus of Nazareth, and of his dying and rising from the grave. The interpretation of the facts is that this took place 'for us men and for our salvation'. In these two simple statements of fact and interpretation we sum up the breadth and depth of biblical revelation.

In referring to the birth of Jesus as *incarnation* we take seriously the biblical assertion that this was no mere man, nor even a man with some divine qualities. The baby in the manger was at one and the same time, in one and the same person, both Son of God *and* son of man – both fully divine *and* fully human; both God *and* man. Without the recognition that Jesus Christ was truly God and truly man we cannot maintain the gospel as good news nor as the power of God for salvation. This is why belief in the incarnation is not merely a theoretical matter. The gospel is saying that, what man cannot do in order to be accepted with God, this God himself has done for us in the person of Jesus Christ. To be acceptable to God we must present to God a life of perfect and unceasing obedience to his will.

The gospel declares that Jesus has done this *for us*. For God to be righteous he must deal with our sin. This also he has done *for us* in Jesus. The holy law of God was lived out perfectly *for us* by Christ, and its penalty was paid perfectly for us by Christ. This living and dying of Christ *for us*, and this alone is the basis of our acceptance with God.

Only the God-Man Jesus Christ could both live the true sinless human life and rise victorious over death after paying the penalty for man's sin. We cannot understand how the one person, Jesus Christ, contained two distinguishable yet inseparable natures. No more could the apostles understand it, yet they were driven to accept the fact as integral to the gospel. About this we shall have more to say later.

To sum up: the gospel is what God has done for us in Christ for our salvation. And as the two natures of this Christ must be distinguished, so also we must distinguish what God does *for us* and what God does *in us*. Likewise, as we must not separate the two natures of Christ, neither must we separate the gospel from the fruit of the gospel. It is by the gospel that we are born again (I Peter 1: 23–25), it is the gospel that evokes true faith (Romans 10: 17), and it is the gospel which produces the sanctified or Spirit-filled life (Colossians 1: 56).[1] Now, somehow all this is related to the Old Testament, and we must try to understand how.

THE GOSPEL OF THE KINGDOM

The gospel is sometimes referred to as 'the gospel of the kingdom' (Matthew 4: 23, 9: 35, 24: 14). Mark informs us that Jesus preached the gospel of God by declaring that 'the kingdom of God is at hand' (Mark 1: 14–15). The theme of the gospel has to do with the Kingdom, and this idea of Kingdom is not something completely new – it is 'at hand' because the 'time is fulfilled'. What is more, the term 'kingdom of God' must have meant something to those who heard Jesus even though it is not of itself an Old Testament term.[2]

The unavoidable conclusion from the New Testament evidence is that the gospel fulfils the Old Testament hope of the coming of the Kingdom of God. But we must be more specific about what this means and how it is worked out in the New Testament itself. We have looked at the Kingdom idea in the Old Testament as it is expressed in three distinct yet related epochs or strata – Eden, Israel's history, and prophetic futurism. If the gospel fulfils the expectations of the Kingdom we should be able to discern how this is so by looking at the New Testament evidence. Furthermore, we

---

[1] It will be seen from this that the mystery of the incarnation is of the same order as the mystery of the Trinity – three persons, one God. This is to be expected if Jesus is the supreme revelation of the Triune God. Furthermore, just as we must distinguish but not separate the two natures of Christ, so also we must distinguish but not separate the three persons of the Godhead. To rightly distinguish is to express the unity of the three without confusing them. Thus we must not confuse the Son with the Spirit, not the work of the Son with the work of the Spirit. Hence the need to be clear about the distinctions between God's work for us in the Son, and God's work in us by the Spirit.

[2] The theme of the Kingdom of God as a unifying element in the Bible is discussed by John Bright in *The Kingdom of God* (New York: Abingdon Press, 1955).

are now in a position to clarify one aspect of biblical interpretation. The fact that the various strata of Kingdom revelation in the Bible define the progressive nature of revelation reminds us of the diversity of expression within the overall unity. Each kingdom expression – Eden, Israel, Prophetic Kingdom, and now the Gospel – represents the same reality, but each expresses that reality in a different (yet related) way.

Related – yet different! Each kingdom expression differs from those that preceded it. But many Christians do not understand the implications of this fact. For the New Testament says that the reality is in the gospel – in Christ himself. That is why he must interpret all Scripture. Now some Christians see the implications of their view of the inspiration and authority of Scripture as requiring what they call a literal interpretation of Scripture. But this is not so if by literal is meant that fulfilment must be in the precise terms of the promise, and that the reality is only a future repetition of the foreshadowing.

The New Testament knows nothing of this kind of literalism. It repeatedly maintains that Christ is the fulfilment of these terms, images, promises and foreshadowings in the Old Testament which were presented in a way that is different from the fulfilment. For the New Testament the interpretation of the Old Testament is not 'literal' but 'Christological'. That is to say that the coming of the Christ transforms all the Kingdom terms of the Old Testament into gospel reality.[3] Let us examine this process of transformation in more detail.

THE PEOPLE OF THE KINGDOM

The first element of our Old Testament Kingdom of God was the people of God. In Eden God's people is Adam and Eve.[4] In Israel's

---

[3] Not everything is necessarily changed and obviously literalness remains applicable to some aspects of prophetic fulfilment. Thus messianic prophecies regarding the birth of a child and the place of Bethlehem are fulfilled literally. This literalness is a function of the fact that in order to redeem sinners God enters into the fallen world of sinners. The whole point of the incarnation is that God enters into an intimate relationship with our world through Jesus Christ.

[4] This is not bad grammar! 'People' in Hebrew is a collective singular referring to the nation or race as a single entity thus signifying a solidarity. In modern English usage people often has come to be weakened to a plural of person or individual.

history, the people of God is essentially the descendants of Abraham through Isaac and Jacob. In prophetic hope, the people of God is the faithful remnant of Israel. In the gospel, the people of God is Jesus Christ.

First, Jesus is depicted as *the true Adam* (or last Adam). Consider the following:

Jesus is descended from Adam (Luke 3: 23–38).
Jesus overcomes temptation where Adam failed (Mark 1: 12–13).
Jesus' baptism identifies him with Adam's race (Luke 3: 21–22).
Jesus is the last Adam (Romans 5: 18–21, I Corinthians 15: 20–22; 45–49).
Jesus is the Son of Man (a term meaning human being and thus a member of Adam's race).[5]

Secondly, Jesus is the *seed of Abraham*. On first reading Paul is using unfair tactics when he argues this point in Galatians 3: 16.[6] But Paul's argument comes out of the whole Old Testament background in which the solidarity of the race with its head is to be discerned. Paul is establishing that the seed of Abraham, Israel, has its meaning only in Christ. He alone is the true Israel. The same point is seen in the Gospels. Matthew's genealogy establishes Jesus as the son of Abraham through David (Matthew 1: 1). Thirdly, Jesus is the true Israel. This is but a development on the last point, for Israel is the seed of Abraham. Matthew makes this point when he applies Hosea's backward reference to the exodus – 'out of Egypt have I called my son' – to the return of Jesus, Mary and Joseph after the death of Herod (Matthew 2: 15). Whatever else it may signify, the application of an historical reference concerning Israel to a similar event in Jesus' life must imply some kind of identity to warrant the description of 'fulfilment'. We also note the account of Jesus' temptation in the wilderness (Matthew 4: 1–11, Luke 4: 1–13). Each of the scriptures quoted by Jesus to counter the temptations comes from the early chapters of Deuteronomy which deal with Israel's temptations in the wilderness of Sinai. The

[5] There are numerous references in the Gospel to Jesus as Son of Man. It is certain that many of them link Jesus to Adam via the vision of Daniel 7 where the figure is not only human but also heavenly.

[6] 'Now the promises were made to Abraham and his offspring. It does not say "And to offsprings" referring to many; but referring to one, "And to your offspring", which is Christ.'

implication is that where old Israel was tempted and failed, Jesus (the true Israel) overcomes.

Fourthly, Jesus is the *Son of David*. The promise God made to Abraham's descendants was frequently summarized with the great covenant formula, 'I will be their God, they shall be my people'. In II Samuel 7: 14 the son of David has this promise applied to him in a personal way, 'I will be his father, he shall be my son.' The solidarity between leader and people is again expressed. The king embodies the whole people and is their representative.

These various identities of Jesus establish one clear point. Jesus Christ is the head of the new race. All who are united to him are members of that race, but only because he *is* that race. Thus whoever is 'in Christ' is a new creation (II Corinthians 5: 17), that is, he belongs to the new order of which Christ is head.

THE LOCATION OF THE KINGDOM

The second element of our Old Testament kingdom we called 'God's place'. This may be a less than satisfactory way of describing the New Testament idea of kingdom which is not confined to such a strict spatial concept as a garden (Eden) or a land (Israel) –though it continues to employ Old Testament terms from time to time. Nevertheless we must find some way to convey the sense of 'place' in the New Testament.

In our first stratum of revelation the place of the kingdom was *Eden*, and in the second it was the *land of Canaan*. Since both are presented as part of this created earth, there is a predictable area of continuity between them despite the fact that one belongs to the period before and the other to the period after the Fall. The third stratum, the prophetic futurist kingdom, adapts the Canaan model of kingdom location but 'glorifies' it. As we have already seen, there emerges in some prophetic predictions a clear mixing of elements which belong to both the previous strata – Eden and Israel's Canaan.

In the Old Testament salvation includes a restoration of God's people into the environment which best fits their restored relationship with God. As Eden represented the perfection of the first creation so the redemptive process entails a remaking of the Eden-paradise. This progression of imagery may thus be summarized as the garden paradise in the beginning, the land 'flowing with milk and honey' in Israel's history, and the new heavens and earth with a new paradise in the prophetic view.

The New Testament continues this progression. Jesus declares his kingdom is not of this world (John 18: 36), yet at the same time the earthly Old Testament images are repeated but with greater clarity. Peter repeats Isaiah's prediction of a new heaven and earth but says it represents such a complete break with things as they are now that this present order must pass away (II Peter 3: 10–13). The Old Testament develops the 'Israel' stratum by focusing on Jerusalem (*Zion*) as the centre of God's land. Thus the prophets often depict the restoration of Zion as the manifestation of the kingdom of God. It is to Zion that the returning faithful remnant come, and likewise it is to Zion that the Gentiles come who are being drawn into the kingdom.

Now, if Israel's hope was that the nation would return to Zion (for example Isaiah 35: 10) we must enquire of the New Testament where Zion is to be found. Hebrews 12: 22 indicates that a Jew comes to Zion by being converted to Christ. Zion is *where Jesus reigns now* at the right hand of God and this is where we come by faith in the gospel.

Another important passage is Hebrews 11: 8–16. Here the theme is the inheritance of God's people, in this case Abraham and the patriarchs. From the interpretative standpoint of the gospel the writer can describe Abraham's hope in gospel terms – he looked forward to the city which has foundations, whose builder and maker is God (verse 10). Of the patriarchs' hope he maintains that they desired a better country, that is, a heavenly one (verse 16). It is the gospel which enables the writer to trans-form the Old Testament image, which is bound to this old order, into an aspect of the new order. One other important focal point in the locality of God's kingdom is the Temple. The Temple could function as such a focal point because it represented the dwelling of God among his people. It demonstrated that the promised land was not merely living space for people but was the setting for a relationship between God and man. The Temple was thus integral to the existence of the Kingdom of God and by it the Kingdom could be identified.

The use made of the Temple theme in the New Testament is vital to our understanding of the relationship of Old and New Testaments. One thing is clear: the New Testament declares that the new Temple has already come into existence, for it is none other than Jesus Christ. John describes the incarnation thus: 'The Word was made flesh and dwelt among us' (John 1: 14). The literal translation of the Greek is '. . . and *tabernacled* among us'. In other words, John saw Jesus as resembling the tabernacle in the wilderness. Why is Jesus the Temple? Because he is God dwelling among us.

But the idea is developed even further: Jesus is God and man in closest union. The very being of Jesus is the most perfect relationship of God and man. Thus when Jesus disputes with the Jews over his cleansing of the Temple (John 2: 13–22) he proposes as a sign of his authority: 'Destroy this temple and in three days I will raise it up' (verse 19). His opponents are obsessed by the old order and can think only of the bricks and mortar of Herod's temple. But John tells us that Jesus was referring to his own body as the Temple so that it was his resurrection from the dead which gave the disciples the key to what he had said (verse 22).

These images of locality – garden, land, city, temple – all reach their fulfilment in the gospel. For the New Testament the locality of the Kingdom is Jesus Christ himself. And, lest we be misled by a misplaced and unbiblical emphasis, Jesus Christ is shown as risen and seated on the right hand of God in the heavenly places.[7]

THE RULE OF THE KINGDOM

The third element in our Old Testament kingdom pattern is the rule of God over his people by his word. The different covenants of the Bible all testify to this in their own contexts. We may discern two important aspects of this covenant rule of God – the covenants themselves and the mediator of the covenant.

We have already seen how God ruled in Eden by the word which defined Adam's freedom. As for Abraham, not only did God call him, direct him, and make promises to him; the goal of it all was the relationship expressed in the great covenant summary 'I will be your God, you shall be my people'. Later, when Israel understood itself as God's people, this was expressed in the covenant of Sinai which defined the role of God's people in terms of daily living.

[7] It is necessary to stress this fact because of the frequent emphasis given in popular preaching and piety to Christ as enthroned in the heart of the believer. This way of speaking has biblical support (Galatians 2: 20, Ephesians 3: 17, Colossians 1: 27), but must be understood in the light of the biblical emphasis on Christ risen above and coming to us by the Holy Spirit.

Later still, the prophetic hope saw not a different covenant ruling the restored people, but a newly applied covenant – written upon men's hearts – so that there would be a perfect compliance with God's character and will (Jeremiah 31: 31–34).

References to covenant as such are fairly infrequent in the New Testament but there is plenty to show that the gospel is the fulfilment of the hope of the new covenant. The song of Mary is an example of the interpretation of the coming of Jesus as Old Testament hope come to fruition (Luke 1: 46–55). Likewise the songs of Zechariah and Simeon interpret the incarnation in Old Testament terms of covenant (Luke 1: 68–79, 2: 29–32). At the last supper Jesus declares that the cup 'is the new covenant in my blood', thus indicating that his death establishes the reality of the new covenant just as the old covenant was sealed with sacrificial blood by Moses (I Corinthians 11: 25; cf. Exodus 24: 8).

The most detailed exposition of the gospel as the new covenant of Jeremiah is given in Hebrews 8–9. In saying, as the writer does, that the new covenant is so much better than the old which has become obsolete, he in no way implies that old is unconnected with the new. In fact, he establishes the new by showing how it achieves perfectly what the old could only foreshadow. Those who see a radical discontinuity between old and new often support their position with such statements as, 'You are not under law but under grace' (Romans 6: 14). We have already dealt with the law as covenant – a fact established by Jeremiah 31: 31–34 – so New Testament references to the place of law are important. The proper context of such passages showing distinction are those which show unity. Jesus came not to destroy the law but to fulfil it (Matthew 5: 17–20). The law remains the standard of God's righteousness (Romans 2: 13), and faith does not overthrow the law but upholds it (Romans 3: 31). Thus it was to fulfil the demands and the penalty of the law that Jesus lived and died for us. The fact that we cannot do it ourselves does not remove the demand, and if we believe Christ did it for us we uphold the demand.

The other main theme relating to God's rule is the concept of kingship. The judges in Israel are forerunners to the king in some regards but it is with David that the significance of this mediation of God's rule emerges. The pattern of kingship is given in Deuteronomy 17: 14–20 in which we see the king as the mediator of the covenant. In II Samuel 7 the kingly rule is seen in relationship to the Temple so that throne and Temple become almost synonymous in their significance.

How then does the New Testament take up the hope of the restoration of the rule of David in the Kingdom of God? Firstly, by showing that Jesus is the Son of David who by implication will rule in God's Kingdom forever. Secondly, by showing that the fulfilment of the prophecies concerning David's restored rule occurred at the resurrection: 'Being therefore a prophet, and knowing that God had sworn with an oath to him that he would set one of his descendants upon his throne he foresaw and spoke of the resurrection of the Christ.' (Acts 2: 30–31, 36). 'And as for the fact that he raised him from the dead, no more to return to corruption, he spoke in this way, "I will give you the holy and sure blessings of David" ' (Acts 13: 34).

We have already mentioned the Temple in relation to the place of God's kingdom. Now we note that the whole use of this 'temple' theme in the New Testament indicates that in the gospel the Kingdom of God comes to its fulfilment. It was as a sign that God dwelt amongst his people to rule that the holy of holies in the tabernacle contained the ark of the covenant inside which was the written law (Exodus 25: 21–22). Solomon's temple prefigured the fulfilment of the promises to David concerning the rule of David's son given in II Samuel 7. Ezekiel focused on the new temple as the sign of God's ruling and life-giving presence in the kingdom (Ezekiel 47: 1-12). Zechariah saw a new temple built by David's descendant Zerubbabel through the Spirit (Zechariah 4: 6). For John the true temple is the bodily presence of Jesus the 'Logos' or Word (John 1: 14, 2: 21). Stephen understands the need to let go of the man-built temple and to move out to the gospel fulfilment. To hang on to the old is to resist the Holy Spirit (Acts 7: 46-51). For Paul the temple is fulfilled both in the resurrection of Christ (Acts 13: 34; cf. Ephesians 2: 6), and in the presence of Christ through the Holy Spirit (Ephesians 2: 18–22, I Corinthians 3: 16, II Corinthians 6: 16). Peter also sees both the heavenly Temple (Acts 2: 30–31) and the earthly creation of the Spirit (I Peter 2: 4–8). The climax comes in Revelation 21 and 22 where we see the heavenly reality as the ultimate point of reference. Here God himself is the Temple so there is no need for symbolic structures (Revelation 21: 22). Also we see the throne of God in the place of the Temple in Ezekiel's vision (Ezekiel 47) from which flows the river of life (Revelation 22: 1–5). Temple theology is fulfilled through the gospel, the goal of which is aptly stated by the heavenly voice: 'Behold the dwelling of God is with men. He will dwell with them, and they shall be his people' (Revelation 21: 3).

THE KINGDOM: NOW AND NOT YET

Can we say that all Old Testament prophetic hope is fulfilled in the gospel, if that gospel is anchored to historical events that happened two thousand years ago? We cannot simply ignore the second coming of Christ and the promise this holds of a glorious transformation for believers. What about the promised 'end of the world' and the events before and after it? To put it another way: how do we relate the present reality of salvation for the believer to the final revealing of the Kingdom of God in all its glory? Many people in effect regard the second coming of Christ as involving a whole new work of God. This conclusion is forced upon them because they do not accept that all promise is fulfilled in the gospel. Thus, despite the scriptural evidence (cited above) to the contrary, they see the return of Israel, the rebuilding of the Temple, the restoration of Davidic kingship as unrelated to the gospel and requiring separate fulfilment on some future occasion.

If the argument of this book is valid we must conclude otherwise. The New Testament portrays the 'Christ event', which happened two thousand years ago, as the finished, perfect work of God for the salvation of all his people, both Jew and gentile. The gospel – the first coming of Christ – wins for believers all the riches of glory. The acceptance of the believer with God is perfect the moment he believes because Christ and his work are perfect. The status of the believer can never be improved upon – he possesses all the riches of Christ. There is nothing the believer will possess in glory that he does not now possess *in Christ*. All this he possesses *by faith*, but that it is by faith does not make it any less real.

The Christian thus lives in tension between the *now* of living 'by faith' and the *not yet* of knowing the full reality of the kingdom 'by sight'.[8]

One implication of what we are saying is that the Book of Revelation, for many an object of puzzlement, for others a stimulus to wild speculation about the future, is to be interpreted by the gospel. We must also say that the first coming of Christ interprets the second coming. For the believer the second coming of Christ

---

[8] 'The gospel must determine our view of eschatology. The reason is this: the gospel is the report about the 'finished work of Christ'. And if 'the finished work of Christ' is a reality rather than an empty slogan, it means that the last things are simply an unveiling of what has already been done.' R.D. Brinsmead, 'Eschatology in the light of the Gospel', *Present Truth*, Vol. 3, number 4, Sept. 1974, p. 4.

will be the manifestation of his glory and of the glory of his kingdom, a glory which we already grasp by faith. For the unbeliever the second coming will be a manifestation of judgement, which judgement already rests on all sinners even though they do not acknowledge it.[9]

CHRIST THE KINGDOM

When we begin to put all the pieces together, so that we can see the way the overall pattern of Old Testament revelation is handled in the New Testament, a frequently overlooked truth emerges. To see the kingdom of God we must look at Jesus Christ. This is not an inert cliché of pious jargon but it has some important implications for the way we handle the Bible.

We have defined the Kingdom of God as God's people in God's place under God's rule. Now we discover that the New Testament sees the primary point of reference for each of these aspects in the Person of Jesus Christ. He is the true people of God, the true kingly sphere, and the true rule of God.

This brings us back to the starting point in biblical theology referred to in Chapter Four. As Christians we recognise Christ to be the way to God and we believe the gospel of Christ to be the power of God for salvation. Viewed in the light of the whole unity of Scripture, these well-worn phrases take on a depth of meaning that may previously have escaped us. Biblical theology shows us the process of revelation in the Bible leading to the fulfilment of all hope in Jesus Christ. Since Christ is the goal to which all revelation points he, himself, in his person and acts, is the key to the interpretation of all scripture.

---

[9] It will be seen that this discussion implies radical disagreement with some popular teachings on prophecy. While controversy is not the aim of this book, many readers will long since have recognized that the system known as Dispensationalism (represented by the Scofield Reference Bible, and its modern derivatives (such as Hal Lindsey's *The Late Great Planet Earth*) have given a very different understanding of prophetic fulfilment. I only ask those who disagree with me to give my case a fair hearing in the light of scripture, and not to reject it simply because it puts across cherished beliefs. It is of interest to me that Hal Lindsey in *The Late Great Planet Earth* all but ignores the mass of material in the New Testament which deals with the fulfilment in the gospel of the prophecies concerning Israel.

FIG. 7 THE KINGDOM OF GOD AND THE GOSPEL

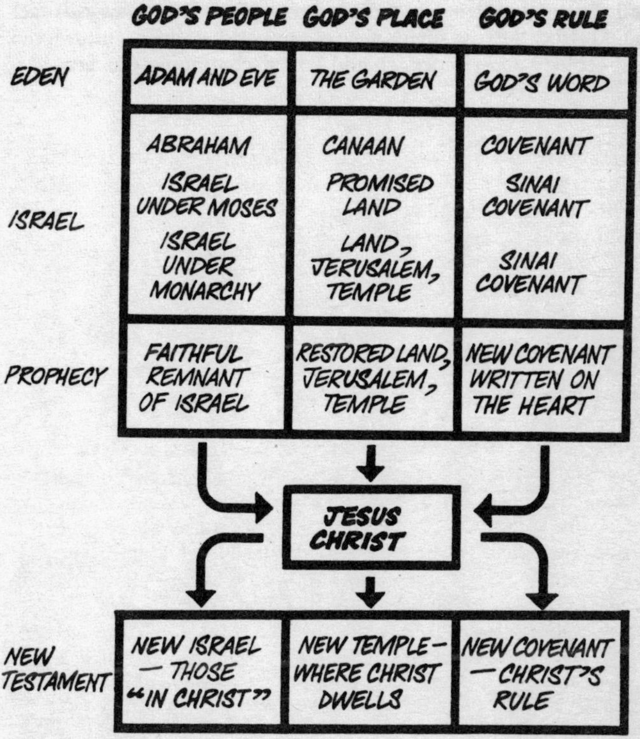

	GOD'S PEOPLE	GOD'S PLACE	GOD'S RULE
EDEN	ADAM AND EVE	THE GARDEN	GOD'S WORD
ISRAEL	ABRAHAM / ISRAEL UNDER MOSES / ISRAEL UNDER MONARCHY	CANAAN / PROMISED LAND / LAND, JERUSALEM, TEMPLE	COVENANT / SINAI COVENANT / SINAI COVENANT
PROPHECY	FAITHFUL REMNANT OF ISRAEL	RESTORED LAND, JERUSALEM, TEMPLE	NEW COVENANT WRITTEN ON THE HEART
		JESUS CHRIST	
NEW TESTAMENT	NEW ISRAEL —THOSE "IN CHRIST"	NEW TEMPLE— WHERE CHRIST DWELLS	NEW COVENANT —CHRIST'S RULE

We conclude this part of the discussion by making one final point. Jesus Christ (as we have seen) contains in himself the Kingdom of God. The gospel is a gospel of man restored to proper relationships in Christ. Now, these relationships involve the whole of reality: God, man, and the created order. As Eden and Canaan are in Christ, so God's perfect world is in Christ. This truth has one vital implication often forgotten by evangelicals, but which the Old Testament reinforces by its historicity. The gospel is not simply 'forgiveness of sins' and 'going to heaven when you die'. The gospel is a restoration of relationships between God, man and the world.

The typology of the Bible and the transformation of Old Testament imagery by the gospel should not be misused to lift us completely outside the created world. The gospel involves us not only with God, but with our fellow men and with the world. How this fact should affect the Christian's view of the world, politics, culture, the arts, ecology and science, should be our continuing concern.

CHAPTER TEN

Principles of Interpretation

IN CHAPTER FOUR, HERMENEUTICS, OR INTERPRETATION, WAS DESCRIBED
as the process of determining how the ancient biblical text has
general relevance here and now. We may now put this a little more
exactly: hermeneutics aims at showing the significance of the text in
the light of the gospel. To interpret an Old Testament text we
establish its relationship to the revelation of God in Jesus Christ. In
order to do this we draw upon our knowledge of the structure of
revelation that biblical theology has opened out for us.

The study of the Kingdom of God concept has shown that each
stratum of Kingdom revelation has the same essential ingredients
relating to the saving acts of God and the goal to which they lead.
Each stratum prefigures the realities of the gospel. Each step is not
only a movement in the chronological sequence of revelation, but is
a movement in the process of making clearer the nature of God's
Kingdom until the full light of the gospel is revealed.

These relationships are shown in the figure on page 100 which
represents both the unity of the whole Bible and the distinctions
between the several strata. In the diagram the boundaries between
the Kingdom epochs are indicated by covenant expressions relating
to the Kingdom. The Kingdom is promised to Abraham and
foreshadowed (typologically fulfilled) with David. The prophets
renew the promise of the Kingdom which is declared to be 'at hand'
with the coming of Christ. At the second coming of Christ the
Kingdom will be fully revealed and consummated.

No diagram can tell the whole story, but this representation at
least provides a basis for interpretation of any Old Testament text.
Our whole study of progressive revelation goes to show that the
Gospel event is the reality which determines all that goes before and
after it.

FIG. 8 **REVELATION OF THE KINGDOM OF GOD**

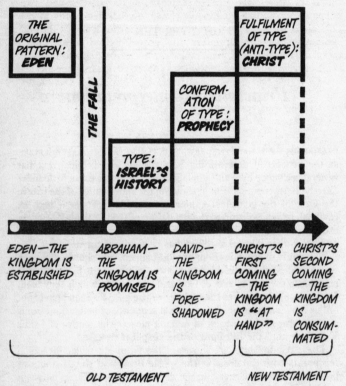

We may look at it another way. From man's point of view we see the Scriptures unfold a step-by-step process until the gospel is reached as the goal. But from God's point of view we know that the coming of Christ to live and to die for sinners was *the* pre-determined factor even before God made the world.[1] We must not think of God as trying first one plan and then another until he came up with the perfect way of salvation. The gospel was pre-ordained so that at the exact and perfect time God sent forth his Son into the world.

[1] Matthew 25: 34, Ephesians 1: 4, 1 Peter 1: 20, Revelation 13:8, 17: 8.

In the meantime, until that perfect 'fulness of time' should be reached, God graciously provided a progressive revelation of the Christ event. These pre-figurements of the gospel had two purposes. First, this progressive revelation led man gently to the full light of truth. Secondly, it provided the means whereby the Old Testament believer embraced the gospel before it was fully revealed. The Old Testament believer who believed the promises of God concerning the shadow was thus enabled to grasp the reality. It was by Christ that the saints of Israel were saved, for such is the unity of the successive stages of revelation that, by embracing the shadow, the believer embraced the reality.

Only in this way can we account for the 'unity expressions' of the New Testament which speak of Old Testament believers as hearing the gospel, seeing Christ, or hoping for a heavenly kingdom.[2] How then may we put this structure of revelation to work for us? Broadly speaking, we do this by showing with what aspect of the gospel revelation the Old Testament text has its essential unity. Already we have seen how we may express each stratum of revelation in terms of the dimensions of the kingdom of God. Every Old Testament text relates in some way to the basic structure of the kingdom revelation and is therefore capable of being related to the New Testament at the corresponding point. Thus a saving event in the Old Testament relates to the one great saving event of the gospel; a priestly mediator of the saving event in the Old relates to the one great priestly mediator of salvation in the gospel, and so on.

THE METHOD IN PRACTICE

We may summarize the process in the following way:

1. Identify the way the text functions in the wider context of the kingdom stratum in which it occurs.
2. Proceed to the same point in each succeeding stratum until the final reality in the gospel is reached.
3. Show how the gospel reality interprets the meaning of the

---

[2] E.g. John 8: 56 – 'Abraham rejoiced to see my day'.

1 Corinthians 10: 4 – 'They drank from the supernatural rock which followed them, and the rock was Christ.'

Galatians 3: 8 – '. . . preached the gospel beforehand to Abraham.'

Hebrews 11: 16 – 'They desire a better country, that is, a heavenly one.'

text, at the same time as showing how the gospel reality is illuminated by the text.

Before offering some examples a few words of warning are indicated. It should be remembered that the structural analysis given in the previous chapters is of the most basic kind. We may not overlook the Old Testament's complexity which calls for care and precision. One aspect of this complexity is the repetition of certain aspects of the structure within one given stratum. Thus, while the exodus is the definitive saving event, every deliverance effected by judge, king or any other means, is a saving event. Another aspect which our diagram does not represent is the significance of the history of Israel after the zenith of the united monarchy. Nor have we said anything yet about those of Israel's faith expressions which do not relate easily to the history of Israel or to prophecy. The wisdom literature has long been a problem to scholars at this point.

A second word of warning relates to our use of the word 'text'. It will, I hope, be evident that by 'text' is not meant simply a single verse of Scripture. It is not possible to lay down rules about how much of the text constitutes an interpretable unit. The lesson of biblical theology is that no text stands alone, and the whole of Scripture is its ultimate context. So we should beware of taking every portion of a size convenient for daily reading (whatever that might be) and forcing it to yield up some self-contained Christian truth. In our efforts to make every snippet of Scripture revelant and edifying to the Christian we may in fact destroy the very message which is present for us in the wider context.

Despite the difficulties mentioned, the gospel and the whole witness of the New Testament should inspire us with confidence that the task can be done. It requires hard work and application, but our efforts will be rewarded as we achieve a clearer understanding of the riches of the gospel.

CHAPTER ELEVEN

It's That Giant Again!

IT IS TIME NOW TO SEE OUR PRINCIPLES PUT INTO PRACTICE. IN THIS chapter we shall look at some Old Testament passages and consider the application of christological interpretation methods. Provided we do not regard these principles as a kind of magic key to every difficulty, and provided we are prepared to work hard at the business of understanding the text, we should be able to avoid the hit-and-miss of so much handling of the Old Testament and to move in the right direction.

DAVID AND GOLIATH: I SAMUEL 17

In Chapter Two we considered some points about this famous story in its context of the life of David. We could not do better than to hear Martin Luther on this text:

> When David overcame the great Goliath, there came among the Jewish people the good report and encouraging news that their terrible enemy had been struck down and that they had been rescued and given joy and peace; and they sang and danced and were glad for it (I Samuel 18: 6). Thus this gospel of God or New Testament is a good story and report, sounded forth into all the world by the apostles, telling of a true David who strove with sin, death, and the devil, and overcame them, and thereby rescued all those who were captive in sin, afflicted with death, and overpowered by the devil.[1]

---

[1] *Word and Sacrament* (Philadelphia, Muhlenberg Press, 1960), Luther's Works, American Edition, Vol. 35, p. 358.

The important point to note is that Luther has made the link between the saving acts of God through David and the saving acts of God through Christ. Once we see that connection, it is impossible to use David as a mere model for Christian living since his victory was vicarious and the Israelites could only rejoice in what was won *for* them. In terms of our interpretative principles, we see David's victory as a salvation event in that the existence of the people of God in the promised land was at stake. The gospel interprets this event by showing it as pre-figuring the true saving event of Christ. But David's experience also puts the saving event into an historical situation which helps us to appreciate the New Testament terminology concerning the gospel events.

We must be careful not to make too much of incidental details which belong to the immediate life-situation described in the text. David's taking of food to his brothers in the army hardly demands interpretation any more than the dimensions of Goliath's armour. Some areas of the narrative, on the other hand, spell out what is significant in theological terms (e.g. verses 45–47). Other details form a pattern within the wider con- text which again emerges in the gospel events. David is declared king in God's eyes (I Samuel 16) but is despised, scorned and rejected. He wins his victory at the point where he seems to be about to suffer total defeat, and his people continue a fight against an already defeated foe.

All Old Testament passages which deal with the Lord's battles against Israel's foes must be evaluated in the light of the saving work of God *for* us.

RAHAB'S SCARLET CORD: JOSHUA 2: 15–21, 6: 22–25

One well-worn line of interpretation focuses on the redness of Rahab's cord as a type of the blood of Christ. This is difficult to maintain while the emphasis is merely on the redness of each. But in our desire to be hermeneutically pure we should not over-react. The conquest of Jericho is part of the saving acts of God for Israel, and of his judgement on the godless Canaanites. That Rahab found safety from this judgement and was saved through obeying the instruction to display a sign of identification, has many real parallels to the passover in Egypt. In that sense the tying of an easily-seen coloured cord to the window had saving significance for Rahab, and the fact that she became incorporated in the people of God (Joshua 6: 25) is a type of salvation. It may seem a small distinction, but it is not the redness which establishes the typology, but the saving significance of the event.

The Rahab passage has another important message because it, along with other passages, demonstrates the purpose of God for the gentiles as promised to Abraham in Genesis 12: 3. As examples of gentile converts we have Jethro of Midian and his daughter whom Moses married, Rahab the Canaanite, and Ruth the Moabitess.

THE POLLUTED SPRING: II KINGS 2: 19–22

The healing of the polluted spring at Jericho by the last of the old-order prophets may well stimulate thoughts about the need for the human heart to be cleansed. The question of human moral pollution is of course closely related to salvation – in fact it is inseparable from it. But let us never lose sight of the fact that God does not save us by eradicating our pollution. We are not saved by our changed lives. The changed life is the result of being saved and not the basis of it. The basis of salvation is the perfection in the life and death of Christ presented in our place.

Now the spring of water in the promised land is closely related to Israel's salvation. Jericho was under a curse from the time Joshua destroyed it (see Joshua 6: 17, 26). The city site ceased to have the same significance as the inheritance of Israel which was a fruitful land flowing with milk and honey. This is not an easy passage, but it would appear that sanction is given for a re-inhabiting of Jericho by the prophet's act. The physical sustenance of the people in the promised land is part of the whole salvation process.

The ritual use of salt lies in some obscurity, but apparently indicates cleansing or a break with the past.[2] We may allow that Elisha's act involved redemption of the potentially life-giving spring from under the curse of the ban. Once again we see this as a saving act of God for his people rather than a purifying act *within* the believer. To drink of the purified spring was in itself to partake of the life that God provided for his people. To take of the water of life is to have life itself. The orientation of the pure spring is Christ himself, not the heart of the believer. God graciously provides the pure water of life in the place of the cursed. We should interpret this passage in the light of Christ as the fulfiller of the place where God keeps his people in eternal life. Canaan and all its fruitfulness is in Christ.

[2] See Leviticus 2: 13, Numbers 18: 19, Judges 9: 45, Ezekiel 43: 24.

BLESSING THE CHILD-KILLERS: PSALM 137

This psalm contains one of those difficult imprecatory passages which call down terrible curses from heaven upon the enemy in what appears to be a wholly immoral fashion. Psalm 109: 6–20 is a more extended imprecation which some have sought to excuse by understanding it as the words of the wicked (v. 2) against the psalmist himself. But there are other clear cases which still leave the problem (e.g. Jeremiah 15: 15, 18: 19-23, Psalm 69: 22-28).

Psalm 137 has an easily discernible context. It springs from the agony of the Babylonian exile, when the pious Jew was torn from the promised land and transported to a foreign country to be tormented with memories of the destruction of Jerusalem and the temple. The whole covenant relationship with God and the salvation of the people were called into question.

The theological context of the controversial verses 7–9 is the hope of redress against the enemies of God's people. Whatever the actual form and content of the expressions, the imprecations are cries for God's Kingdom to come. However much we may allow the culture and the times to have conditioned the prayer, it is essentially a longing for the day of vindication, when the coming Kingdom will introduce terrible judgement on all who oppose it. The psalmist was not conditioned by unrealistic notions about the innocence of children, but by a sense of solidarity of all age groups in a sinful mankind. However cruel the destruction of the next generation of Babylonian soldiers may appear to us, it was seen to be integral to the final overthrow of the enemies of God at the coming of his Kingdom.

As we move to the New Testament it is true that a clearer perspective is to be had. The real enemy is not flesh and blood but principalities and powers. On the other hand the New Testament is quite clear that the human enemy whom we must love, will also come under judgement on 'the great and terrible Day of the Lord'. To pray, 'Thy kingdom come', is a solemn thing indeed.

We have not said all that can be said about the moral problem of child-killing. However we may be disposed to interpret the biblical references in the light of the 'primitive' state of Israel's civilization (a dubious concept), the theological perspective must take precedence. It is distasteful to us that Israel slaughtered whole civilian populations during the conquest. But these historical facts as well as the psalmist's imprecations, cannot be interpreted apart from certain salient aspects of biblical revelation. Firstly that

Israel's own moral failure did not disqualify her from being the agent of God's justice, in the same way that godless nations became God's agents against Israel. Secondly, such slaughter and retribution visited by Israel on another at God's command was truly deserved (see Deuteronomy 9: 4–5). Thirdly, while the judgement in the Old Testament takes the form of death, which man naturally sees as the ultimate punishment, the New Testament depicts a far more horrendous fate for the godless. Death by the sword in the Old Testament is only a pale shadow of the eternal judgement on the godless in the New Testament.

NEHEMIAH REBUILDS JERUSALEM: NEHEMIAH 2: 17–4: 23

Some years ago a popular radio Bible session broadcast a sermon on this section of Nehemiah in which the speaker used a well-worn but quite inexcusable method. In order to make this piece of post-exilic history applicable to the Christian, key words were taken, in this case the names of the repaired gates of Jerusalem, and a kind of association of ideas used to lead us to some useful but largely unrelated New Testament truth. So the Horse Gate led us from horses to soldiers and thence to armour, and finally to the putting on of the whole armour of God in Ephesians 6. The Sheep Gate under repair served as a spring- board from which the speaker jumped without apology to the Good Shepherd of John 10.

Now Ephesians 6 and John 10 have important lessons for us, and these lessons may well overlap the meaning of the original Old Testament passage in question. What is at issue here is the method used. Sermons on the Old Testament should demonstrate, and even spell out in explicit terms, the legitimate relationships of the text to the New Testament.

What are the points to watch in this passage from Nehemiah? First, it belongs to the post-exilic reconstruction age which is not one of our principal strata in the structure of biblical revelation. The return from Babylon did not herald the expected fulfilment of prophecy, but it did bring about a shadow fulfilment in which all the ingredients of the kingdom existed, although very imperfectly. Thus we may treat this period as a kind of interim fulfilment in which the nature of the Kingdom of God is clearly discernible, but during which the problems of imperfection and non-fulfilment of the prophetic hope had to be dealt with.

Secondly, the rebuilding of Jerusalem must point to the prophetic hope for the future glorification of the city of Zion, the focal point of God's Kingdom. At the same time its imperfection says something of the 'not yet' as a dimension in the existence of the people of God. Thirdly, it is the whole event which interprets the details and not the other way round. We should be prepared to forego the christianizing of details unless the theological significance of these details can be established with some certainty. If there is a way to Ephesians 6 from this passage it is not by way of the Horse Gate! Rather the resistance to Nehemiah's work which is offered by his enemies highlights the ongoing conflict with godlessness referred to by Paul in Ephesians 6: 10–20.

Conclusion

THIS DISCUSSION HAS BEEN AT RISK THROUGHOUT SIMPLY BECAUSE OF the aim of keeping it to modest proportions. The reader will inevitably – and rightly – feel that many problems have been left untouched. The aim has been only to establish basic principles of interpretation. Underlying the survey has been the conviction that twentieth century evangelical Christians have experienced a radical loss of direction in handling the Old Testament. One of the contributing causes is the severing of evangelicalism from the historical perspectives of the faith. This introduces a vicious circle, because devotion to study of the Old Testament is an important means of preserving the historicity of the gospel. Evangelicals have lost sight not only of biblical history, but of their own historical heritage in the Reformation. By reverting to either allegorical interpretation on the one hand, or to prophetic literalism on the other, some evangelicals have thrown away the hermeneutic gains of the Reformers in favour of a mediaeval approach to the Bible.

The other great contributing factor to modern misuse of the Old Testament is a generation of bad habits in Bible reading. Evangelicals have had a reputation for taking the Bible seriously. But even they have traditionally propagated the idea of the short devotional reading from which a 'blessing from the Lord' must be wrested. Failure to gain this undefined blessing is usually seen to be a function of the spiritual state of the reader rather than of the nature of the text itself. This mentality is almost paralysed by such phenomena as the genealogies of the Bible. Consequently one is unlikely to find genealogy texts included in daily devotional selections! The difficulties of dealing adequately with the Old Testament when this mentality prevails have been amply discussed in the previous pages.

The pivotal point of turning in evangelical thinking which demands close attention is the change that has taken place from the Protestant emphasis upon the objective facts of the gospel in history, to the mediaeval emphasis on the inner life. The evangelical who sees the inward transforming work of the Spirit as the key element of Christianity will soon lose contact with the historic faith and the historic gospel. At the same time he will come to neglect the historical acts of God in the Old Testament. The Christ enthroned in the human heart loses his own incarnate humanity, and the humanity of the Old Testament history will be soon discarded so that the 'inner spiritual' meanings may be applied to the inner spiritual life of the Christian.

The crisis of the Old Testament today is only another form of the crisis of the Protestant faith. Inner-directed Christianity, which reduces the gospel to the level of every other religion of the inner man, might well use a text from the Apocrypha to serve as its own epitaph for the Reformers:

> There are others who are unremembered;
> they are dead, and it is as though they had never existed.
>   (ben Sirah 44: 9)

By contrast, we should think of these fathers of the faith in the way indicated by the writer to the Hebrews (11: 4):

> *They, being dead, yet speak.*

Appendix A

READINGS

These are some suggested readings from the Old Testament which will introduce the reader to some of the salient features and themes. The passages should be read with the outline of Old Testament history in mind, and in the light of the biblical theology discussed in this book.

Basic List

Genesis 1–3, 12–24.	Amos.
Exodus 19–24.	Jeremiah 1–9, 26–44.
Leviticus 1–7, 16, 23, 26.	Lamentations.
Joshua 23–24.	Ezekiel 34–48.
Judges 1–5.	Haggai.
I and II Samuel.	Malachi.
I Kings 4, 8–12.	Psalms 68, 105, 106, 136, 137.
II Kings 16–25.	Proverbs 8–9.
Ezra 1, 7.	Job 1–2.
Nehemiah 1–6, 8.	Daniel

Advanced List

Genesis 37–50.	Micah.
Exodus 1–15, 25–35.	Proverbs 1–7, 10–15.
Deuteronomy 1–12, 26–30.	Job 1–14, 32–33, 38–42.
Joshua 1–12.	Psalms 1–41.
Judges 6–12.	Ezekiel 1–11.
I Kings 16–22.	Ecclesiastes.

II Kings 1–12.
II Chronicles 24–36.
Hosea.
Isaiah 1–39.

Zechariah.
Esther.
Psalms 107–150.

Appendix B

GROUP STUDY QUESTIONS

In order to facilitate the use of this book in group (or private) study, the following questions may be used as a basis for discussion. The members of the group should read carefully the respective chapters before the study hour.

Chapter One

1. What are your greatest difficulties in reading the Old Testament? Why do these difficulties exist for you?
2. Why is it important to study the Old Testament with the New Testament in mind?
3. Consider the implications for Old Testament study of Luke 24: 25–27, 44–47.

Chapter Two

1. Is the Book of Acts normative for us today? If not, why not?
2. What place is there for the character study?
3. How does the content and imagery of Revelation 21: 1–4, and 22: 1–4 help us in understanding the nature of the Bible's unity?

Chapter Three

1. How does a study of literary types assist the understanding of the Bible?
2. Does it matter if the events recorded in Old Testament historical narrative happened or not?

3. What do we mean when we say that the biblical history has a theological purpose? Can we see the outworking of this in Acts 2: 22–36?

Chapter Four

1. What do we mean by the term biblical theology? How does it differ from dogmatic or credal theology?
2. What is meant by progressive revelation?
3. How does the history of redemption figure in Acts 7: 1–53?

Chapter Five

1. What is the Kingdom of God?
2. What do you understand by salvation?
3. How does the Kingdom of God theme relate to the covenant expressions of Genesis 12 and II Samuel 7?

Chapter Six

1. How is the Kingdom of God seen in Eden?
2. What does the Eden story and its sequel tell us about the meaning of grace?
3. How does Paul relate the Adam history to Christ in Romans 5 and I Corinthians 15: 20–26?

Chapter Seven

1. How does the exodus event relate to the promises to Abraham in Genesis?
2. In what sense is the gospel pre-figured in Israel's history?
3. How does the revelation of the Kingdom of God progress from Abraham to Solomon?

Chapter Eight

1. What is the main difference between the message of the old order prophets and the message of the new order prophets?
2. How does the prophetic view of the future kingdom differ from the past historical kingdom in Israel?
3. How do the prophets use past history to describe the future?

Chapter Nine

1. What is the gospel?
2. How does the New Testament handle the relationship of the gospel to the fulfilment of prophecy?
3. What has the Second Coming of Christ to do with prophetic fulfilment?

Chapter Ten

1. What is the difference between a legitimate typology and the allegorical interpretation?
2. What do we mean when we say that prophecy must be interpreted christologically?
3. Why is the New Testament the ultimate source of the principles of interpretation of the Old Testament?

Appendix C

SOME PASSAGES FOR INTERPRETATION

Prepare outlines of Bible Studies or Sunday School lessons on the following passages. Remember the three basic questions put to any text:

1. What did the text mean to the original writer?
2. What does the text mean in the light of the Gospel?
3. What is its specific meaning to me or my hearers now?

(Do not refer to the comments on the following pages until you have attempted your own answers.)

1. Deuteronomy 6: 20–25.   4. Isaiah 21–4.
2. I Samuel 26.   5. Psalm 114.
3. I Kings 18: 17–40.   6. Amos 5: 18–20.

Some more difficult passages for the adventurous:

7. Proverbs 3: 1–12.   9. Ezekiel 1.
8. II Samuel 23: 1–7.   10. Malachi 4.

NOTES AND COMMENTS ON PASSAGES FOR INTERPRETATION

1. Deuteronomy 6: 20–25.

Exegesis must take account of the context of the law-giving as the sequel to the exodus. Note the important relationships which are involved: that of law and grace (or gospel), or that of works and salvation. In verses 20–23 the law is related to the past saving events, while in verses 24–25 the doing of the law is related to the future saving events. Verse 25 should be dealt with in the context of v. 21. Remember that the New Testament also speaks of rewards for good works and denies a place in the Kingdom to those who do not do them (Romans 2: 6–10, I Corinthians 3: 8, II Corinthians 5: 10, Galatians 5: 21, I Corinthians 6: 9–10).

2. *I Samuel 26*

Take care to relate the principal characters to the theological structure. Do not be quick to see examples for ourselves, until the real functions of the characters and events are worked out. Notice how David is guided by theological understanding while Abishai is guided by circumstances. Consider the implications for christology of the continuing humiliation of David before his accession to the throne.

3. *I Kings 18: 17–40*

The historical background of apostasy is important. Note carefully that Elijah's part in the contest is not merely to outdo the Baal prophets' attempt at miracle, but to reinstate the prescription of the law concerning the sacrifice for sins – see v.v. 30–32, 36–37. There is good fodder here for a gospel sermon.

4. *Isaiah 2: 1–4*

Try putting the questions when? where? what? and why? to the text. The hermeneutics rest upon determining the New Testament counterparts to the answers. Probably the most disputed point will be whether the fulfilment takes place from the beginning of the gospel era or only at the end. We can settle this only by clearly establishing when are the latter days, and when the New Testament sees the restoration of Zion and the Temple taking place.

5. *Psalm 114.*

There should be little difficulty in fitting this psalm into its historical and theological contexts. After that it is a matter of determining the mood of the psalm as an expression of the faithful man who recalls the saving acts of God.

6. Amos 5: 18–20

Although this is probably the earliest reference in Scripture to the day of the Lord, the term obviously has a recognised meaning in Amos' time. It would be a good idea to research its meaning with the aid of a concordance. For Amos there is a double significance to this great future event, for it was anticipated as a day of light, but for some it would be darkness. This must be interpreted in the context of the biblical teaching of judgement.

7. Proverbs 3: 1–12

The main obstacle in this kind of passage is the understanding of what the wisdom literature is all about. This is a relatively straightforward 'instruction' passage which belongs to the expressions of faith in the on-going life of the people of God. Essentially wisdom speaks of understanding the relationships of man to man, to the world, and to God. It does so with greater emphasis on the responsible freedom of man to respond to the world than on the revealed saving acts of God. Proverbs 1: 7 reminds us that this freedom is true freedom only while it is exercised within the bounds set by God's revelation. This passage deals directly with wisdom in its theological context, but this should not be allowed to obscure the wisdom stance which is behind the proverbial material such as is in Proverbs 10 and following.

8. II Samuel 23: 1–7

This psalm-like passage, along with Chapter 22, has obviously been placed at the end of the David narratives for a purpose. It highlights the fact that the narrative material is not only biographical or historical but shaped by theological purpose. These last words of David sum up the theological meaning of the covenant of II Samuel 7 and indeed of the whole reign of David. The covenant and reign of David are key elements in the messianic hope developing in the Old Testament. Both the man and his office are idealised here without the qualifications of the historic blemishes. As such they form an important link in the chain of christological reference in the Bible.

9. Ezekiel 1

The historical context is no problem. The literary form may well be influenced by the emergence of apocalyptic. The vision of the 'heavenly locomotive' does not necessarily demand an interpretation of every detail, especially when it is seen as the background to the essential element which is the glory of the Lord. The passage does not really stand on its own, and the progressive departure of the glory of the Lord in Chapters 1 to 11 provides the real key.

10. Malachi 4

Salvation and judgement are the parallel themes in v.v. 1–3. It is verses 4–6 that will probably give most trouble. We may be partly guided by the assertion in Matthew 17: 10–13 that John Baptist is the Elijah spoken of here. Elijah did what the prophet does in v. 4 – he called the people to faithfulness to the covenant. Moses and Elijah thus became symbolic of the righteousness of God as he upholds his own law in salvation. The relationship of law and gospel again emerges as a point to be considered (see Romans 3: 21–31, especially v. 31).

Index

Abraham, 34, 35, 37, 41, 45,
    47, 48, 56–8, 65, 75, 89,
    91, 92, 99, 101, 105
    See also Covenant, Patriarchs
Adam, 34, 44, 46
– last (true), 89
Allegorical interpretation, 15f.,
    17, 25, 109
Apocalyptic, 79, 119

Babylon, 30, 35f., 37, 42, 56,
    77, 79, 81, 107
Bible
– for children, 9–11, 14, 21,
    26
– unity of, 11, 14f., 26–8, 38,
    39, 84, 97f.
    See also New Testament, Old
    Testament, Scripture
Biblical theology, 38, 39f., 54,
    96, 99, 102
Bright, John, 34n.2, n.4, 87n.2

Canaan, Canaanites, 14, 30,
    34n.4, 35, 59, 61, 71, 82,
    90, 104, 105
Captivity, 35, 47, 58–60, 77, 80,
    81
– new, 81
Character study, 24–26
Christology, 70, 85–7, 88, 104,
    105, 117, 118
Church, 9, 15, 16, 17, 23, 39

– dogma of, 15f.
Conversion, 19, 58
Covenant, 44–6, 60–3, 64, 69,
    70f., 82, 93, 99
– at Sinai, 35, 60–4, 70, 75–7,
    81, 82
– new, 81f., 93
– summary formula, 62,
    71n.15, 90, 92
– with Abraham, 35, 46, 47,
    56–8, 61, 62, 65, 73, 75,
    80, 81
– with David, 71, 81f.
Creation, 45, 49ff., 53
– new, 51, 80, 82, 90–1

Daniel, 31n.1, 79
David, 10, 25f., 47, 69–71, 94,
    99–100, 103, 117, 118
Day of the Lord, 47, 82, 106,
    118
Deuteronomy, 62n.7, 63, 65, 89
Dispensationalism, 96n.9
Doctrine, 39, 40

Eden, 34, 44f., 46, 48, 49–55,
    56, 72, 82, 88, 90f., 92, 97,
    100
Egypt, Egyptians, 35, 36, 37,
    42, 46, 64, 72, 81, 104
Elijah, 25, 76, 117, 119
Eschatology, 76, 95
– prophetic, 76–82, 90, 95n.8

Evangelical, 7, 14, 20, 85, 97, 109f.
Exegesis, 43
Exile, 35, 41, 56, 106
See also Captivity
Exodus, 34n.8, 37, 42, 48, 58–60, 61, 67, 81, 102
– Book of, 59, 61, 62
– new, 81
Ezekiel, 47, 77, 79
Ezra and Nehemiah, 82, 108

Faith, 10, 17, 18, 20, 23, 45, 57, 58, 64n.10, 87, 96
See also Justification by Faith
Fall, 34, 44f., 51f., 53, 65

Genealogies, 55, 109
Genesis, 36, 45, 50f., 54, 56, 57
Gentile nations, 78f., 81, 82
God,
– acts of, 20, 32, 37f., 41, 59, 61, 65f., 67, 75, 80, 85, 95, 99, 104
– creator, 34, 44, 49
– knowledge of, 22
– name of, 59
– rule of, 45f., 47, 48, 50f., 52, 57, 66f., 80, 92–8
– sovereignty of, 44, 50, 52, 58, 70
See also Son of God
Goliath, 10, 26, 70, 103, 104
Gospel, 22, 40–2, 45, 47f., 53, 65, 97, 101f., 109f.
– as fulfilment, 48, 87, 93, 95f., 99f.
– definition of, 18, 20f., 65n.12, 85–8, 97
See also Jesus Christ
Gospels, 23f., 42
Grace, 18, 45, 53f., 55, 61f., 64, 75

Hermeneutics, interpretation, 89, 91, 92, 99, 101, 105
hesed, loving-kindness, steadfast love, 65, 67, 81

History, 18, 29, 32–8, 39, 40, 41, 42, 54, 56
Holy Spirit, 23, 26, 86, 87, 92n.7, 94, 110

Image of God, 44f., 50, 53, 84
Imprecations, 106f.
Israel, 24, 35, 45, 58
– history of, 32f., 35–7, 40, 46–7, 55–73, 74, 80, 82, 89, 100, 102
– new, 81, 89
– hope of, 42, 87

Jacob, 35, 41, 58
Jericho, 66, 105
Jerusalem, Zion, 17, 35, 42, 78, 80, 106, 107f.
– new, 51, 82
Jesus Christ
– as hermeneutic principle, 18, 85, 86, 89, 96, 99–101, 104
– death of, 23, 86, 93
– fulfiller and goal of prophecy, 19f., 41, 42, 47–8, 84–98, 100, 105
– image of God, 50
– incarnation, 29, 86, 91f., 110
– life of, 18, 23, 86, 93
– person and work, 18, 26, 86f., 97, 100
– resurrection and ascension, 23, 24, 86, 92, 94, 95
– revealer of Kingdom, 47f., 84–98
– second coming, 23, 95f.
Jews, 24, 30, 35, 41f., 47, 82, 91, 106
Joshua, 64
– Book of, 66
Judah, 33, 35, 73, 74, 77, 81, 82
Judaism, 42, 82–3
Judges, 26, 66f., 70, 93, 102
– Book of, 26, 66f.

Judgement, 44, 51, 52f., 67, 77f., 79, 96, 106f., 118f.
Justification by Faith, 18, 57n.2, 61, 95

Kingdom of God, 41, 42, 99, 106, 108
See also under Table of Contents

Law, 31, 36, 40, 60–4, 68, 75, 76f., 94
 – and gospel, 60, 61, 62, 65, 86, 93f., 116, 119
Lindsey, Hal, 96n.9
Literalism, 32, 47, 88, 109
Literature and literary types, 9, 30–2, 39
Luther, Martin, 103f.

Man, 45, 50, 51–5
Messiah, Lord's anointed, 24, 26, 42, 69f., 84, 118
Middle ages, mediaeval, 15f., 28, 109f.
Monarchy, kingship, 41, 42, 46, 47, 67–73, 80, 94, 102
Moses, 25f., 30, 31, 33, 35, 40, 41, 58–61, 64, 68, 75, 76, 93, 105, 119

New heaven and new earth, 82, 91
New Testament,
 – fulfilment of Old Testament, 41, 42, 85, 96, 97, 101
 – use of Old Testament, 00
Noth, Martin, 34n.4
Numbers, Book of, 64

Old Testament
 – dimensions of, 30–8
 – history in, 32–8
 – interpretation of, 20
 – Jesus' atttitude to, 20
 – problem of, 12f., 22f., 26, 28
 – reading of,
 – relationship to N.T., 12f., 19

Patriarchs, 12, 15f., 17–20, 24, 41, 42, 61, 84, 85, 87, 88, 93, 97, 101, 107
Paul, 19, 22f., 28, 57n.1, n.2
Pentecost, 23, 86
People of God, 42, 45, 46, 51–7, 63f., 88–90, 96, 97, 118
Peter, 86
Pharisees, 47, 83
Philistines, 68, 70
Priest, 63, 101
Promise and fulfilment, 19, 41, 42, 47, 48, 56–60, 61, 66, 71f., 87–90, 95f., 99, 108
See also Covenant
Promised Land, 35, 46, 56–8, 64–6, 67, 80
 – new land, 80, 90–2
Prophecy, 31, 48, 80–2, 89, 91, 100
Prophets, 26, 41, 47, 75, 76, 84, 99
 – old order, 68, 69, 71, 74–6, 105
 – Pre-exilic, 76–9, 81
 – exilic and post-exilic, 79–83
Protestant, 17f., 110

Rahab, 104f.
Redemption, 28, 46f., 59
 – history of, 18, 20, 41, 42, 46, 47, 58, 65, 84
Reformation, 17f., 109f.
Regeneration, new birth, 20, 65n.12, 87
Remnant, 65, 83
Revelation, 18, 22, 37f., 48f., 67, 73, 88, 96, 99f., 107, 118

Salvation, 17, 20, 40, 55, 56, 61, 62, 67, 69, 75, 78, 80f., 82, 90, 95, 96, 100, 101, 104, 119

– history of, 18, 20, 32, 56,
  65, 70
Samuel, 68–9, 76
Santification, holiness, 20, 63–4,
  65n.12, 87
Saul, 35, 68–9
Scripture
  – application of, 9–11, 23,
    24f., 103, 107
  – authority of, 49, 88
  – four-fold meaning of, 15f.
  – inspiration of, 9, 12f., 88
  – reading of, 8, 10, 11, 26,
    102, 109, 111
  – text of, 22f., 27f., 39f.,
    42f., 99, 102
Sin, sinners, 10, 20, 34, 40, 44,
  45, 46, 51f., 53, 55, 63, 67,
  77, 78, 80, 81, 86
Sinai, 35, 60f., 68
  See also Covenant
Solomon, 35, 47, 71–3, 75, 80
Son of David, 71, 90, 94
Son of God, 71, 85, 86
Son of Man, 86, 89

Stepehn Langton, 15n.1
Sunday School, 9–11, 14, 26

Tabernacle, 63f., 71, 92, 94
Temple, 35, 47, 71, 72, 73, 80,
  82, 91f., 93f., 106
  – new, 81, 91f., 93f.
Theology, 18, 22, 30, 37f., 39f.
Thomas, W. Ian, 15n.1
Trinity, 87n.1
Typology, foreshadowing,
  pattern, pre-figuring, 48,
  69, 70, 73, 82, 94, 98, 99,
  101, 104, 105, 107f

Unity and distinction (diversity),
  28, 38, 80, 85f., 87, 93, 94,
  99, 100

Wisdom, 72, 102, 118
Word of God, 25, 28, 37f., 44,
  49f., 51, 69, 92, 94
Works, 61–4, 75, 116

Zion, 47, 81
  – new, 81, 91, 117